Happy

Dec '92

The Advanced Guide to
CAKE DECORATING

The Advanced Guide to
CAKE DECORATING

WH SMITH

EXCLUSIVE
· BOOKS ·

ACKNOWLEDGEMENTS

The publishers would like to thank the following authors whose contributions have made this a most authoritative reference book on advanced cake decorating skills.

Pat Ashby (Marzipan); Norma Laver (Piping); Nicholas Lodge (Lace and Filigree; Pastillage & Sugar Moulding; Sugar Flowers); Brenda Purton (Royal Icing); and Anne Smith (Sugarpaste).

This edition published 1992 by W H Smith Limited
by arrangement with
Merehurst Limited, Ferry House, 51-57 Lacy Road, Putney, London SW15 1PR

© Copyright 1992 Merehurst Limited

A catalogue record for this book is available from The British Library

ISBN 1-85391-297-2

Edited by Barbara Croxford
Designed by Maggie Aldred
Photography by Graham Tann and Melvin Grey

Typeset by BMD Graphics Limited, Hemel Hempstead
Colour separation by Fotographics Ltd, UK - Hong Kong
Printed in Hong Kong by Leefung-Asco Printers Ltd

Notes on using the recipes

A standard spoon measurement is used for all recipes
1 teaspoon = one 5 ml spoon
1 tablespoon = one 15 ml spoon
All spoon measures are level.
Quantities are given in metric, Imperial and cups. Follow one set of measures only as they are not interchangeable. American terms have been included as necessary throughout, given in brackets following the UK name.

COMPARISONS FOR AMERICAN READERS

caster sugar	superfine sugar
cocktail stick	toothpick
cornflour	cornstarch
greaseproof paper	wax paper
icing sugar	confectioner's sugar
muslin	cheesecloth
palette knife	metal spatula
white fat	shortening

CONTENTS

Introduction 7

BACK TO BASICS 8-15
Marzipanning 9-11
Making and applying royal icing and sugarpaste 12-14
Using a piping bag 15

SIMPLE DECORATIONS 16-35
Crimping, embossing and ribbon insertion 17-19
Garrett frill and broderie anglaise 20-23
Painting on sugarpaste 24-29
Cutwork 30-35

ROYAL ICING WORK 36-47
Brush embroidery 37
Basic and pressure piping 38-41
Basic and tube embroidery 42-45
Lettering 46-47

ADVANCED ROYAL ICING 48-87
Runout work 49-55
Extension and tulle work 56-61
Lace 62-73
Filigree 74-83
Oriental stringwork 84-87

MODELLING 88-127
Marzipan 90-97
Sugarpaste 98-105
Making moulds 106-113
Pastillage greetings cards 114-116
Bas relief 118-127

SUGAR FLOWERS 128-159
Piped flowers 129-139
Flower baskets 136-139
Moulded flowers 140-159
Bouquets and sprays 154-157

Index 160

INTRODUCTION

Cake decorating is a fascinating and popular craft that can be enjoyed by people of all ages and ability. Although this book is primarily aimed at the more advanced cake decorator, it is not designed to exclude those who are just beginning to appreciate the craft. I have learned from my own students that they enjoy collecting books that they feel, at the time, are beyond their capabilities so they have a goal to aim for. They soon learn that with continued practise, perseverance and gradual confidence in their ability these skills are attainable. I therefore hope that all cake decorators, regardless of their ability, will enjoy the challenges throughout the book and it will inspire them to new heights of creativity and skill. The book initially deals with basic recipes and essential techniques to stimulate the beginner and act as a refresher course for the enthusiast. The section on Simple Decorations highlights in detail skills including those using crimpers, embroidery anglaise, ribbon insertion, Garrett frills and the application of colour to the cake surface by painting. Marzipan is a very undervalued medium and has many more uses than simply covering a cake as the decorations using cut-work and inlaid work show.

Royal icing is covered in great depth from simple piping to advanced lace, filigree and bridge extension work. Although the intricate borders, runout collars and fine lace work look daunting, with practise and patience it is possible to master the skill of piping which is so essentail for applying the finished details to most cakes.

The art of pastillage, modelling and bas relief is very popular and can be enormous fun. In its most simplistic form, it can even be a source of inspiration to children who have wonderful, yet basic ideas and love to 'help' to decorate a cake or make moulded and modelled decorations for the Christmas tree.

The final chapter of the book deals with the creation of beautifully modelled sugar flowers and foliage and their formation into sprays, corsages and bouquets. As the art of sugarcraft has developed, the formation of flowers has improved and they are now amazingly realistic and botanically accurate in their construction and colouring, creating quite remarkable, lifelike results.

It is hoped that decorators will be inspired to use their own creative ability and skills to stimulate their imagination, selecting ideas and techniques illustrated in detail throughout the book to create something that is original and personal.

I am proud to have contributed to this book as I know my colleagues are and I hope that it will be a source of pleasure and enjoyment essential in the continuing development of sugarcraft.

Anne Smith

BACK TO BASICS

For beautiful finished cakes, the basic techniques of marzipanning and icing a cake must always be carried out well. All experienced cake decorators know that a good icing surface is essential for perfect results.

Pink birthday cake: This round pink cake is suitable for a birthday or other occasion.

Cover the cake with pale pink sugarpaste. Make the pinks following the instructions for carnations, but cut with a medium-sized primula cutter. Before attaching the petals, paint or dust the inside with dark pink colouring, as it will be impossible to do so when the flower is assembled. To make buds, place a piece of pink paste in a cone of green paste, attach onto wire and mould to shape. Cut the top with a modelling knife to give the effect of an opening bud. Attach the flowers to the cake. Roll out some long, thin pieces of green paste for stems and attach to the cake surface with a little egg white or clear alcohol. Make foliage from curled strips of paste. Make a glue from green flower paste mixed with egg white, and attach the pinks to the cake. Add a sugarpaste label. Finish off with embroidery, a small snailstrail and ribbon round the base. (For carnations, see page 141.)

Marzipan Recipes

Bought white and yellow marzipan is readily available and most popular with cake decorators. However, this recipe for a homemade version is ideal for most sugarcraft work.

Makes about 350g (12oz)
200g (7oz/1¾ cups) sugar
120ml (4fl oz/½ cup) water
pinch cream of tartar
150g (5oz/1¼ cups) ground almonds
1-2 drops almond essence or extract
1 large egg white
icing (confectioner's) sugar, for dusting

Put the sugar and water in a small saucepan and cook over low heat, stirring occasionally, until the sugar is dissolved.

Add the cream of tartar and quickly bring to the boil. Boil until it reaches a temperature of 116°C (240°F), or soft ball stage.

Remove from the heat and beat until the mixture turns cloudy. Add the ground almonds and the almond essence. Whisk the egg white lightly and add to the pan. Return the pan to low heat and cook for 2 minutes, stirring constantly.

Lightly dust a board or work surface with icing sugar and turn out the paste. Cover and leave until cold.

Knead the paste for 2-3 minutes, or until it is completely smooth and free of cracks. Wrap in a plastic bag and store in a cool dry place.

Uncooked Marzipan

This marzipan is excellent for modelling.

450g (1lb/4 cups) icing sugar
250g (8oz/2 cups) ground almonds
2 egg whites, lightly beaten

Sift the icing (confectioner's) sugar into a bowl with the ground almonds.

Make a well in the centre and add the lightly beaten egg white. Stir together to form a firm paste. Knead until smooth.

Always dust the work surface with icing sugar, never flour or cornflour. Roll out the marzipan with a rolling pin. Prevent it from sticking by lifting and rotating it, but do not turn it over.

When marzipanning a cake for sugarpaste, carefully pick up the marzipan by draping it over the rolling pin.

Doris pinks made by the same technique for carnations on page 141.

Marzipanning a Cake for Sugarpaste

A sugarpasted cake must have smooth rounded edges and corners. To achieve this, the marzipan is applied in one piece.

Applying marzipan

Knead the marzipan until pliable.

Knead on a clean dry work surface with a circular motion so that the edge of the paste is brought into the middle, forming pleats. The lower surface remains quite smooth. When rolling out, this smooth side should be uppermost.

Roll out on a surface evenly dusted with icing sugar. Never use flour or cornflour as these can

Gently heat some apricot jam purée and brush over the surface of the cake to ensure that the marzipan will stick.

cause fermentation.

Keep the marzipan moving so it does not stick but don't turn it over. Roll out to the shape of the cake. The use of marzipan spacers at this stage ensures that the overall thickness of the marzipan is constant.

Measure the cake with a piece of string; up one side, across the top and down the other side. The marzipan should be rolled out a little larger than this measurement.

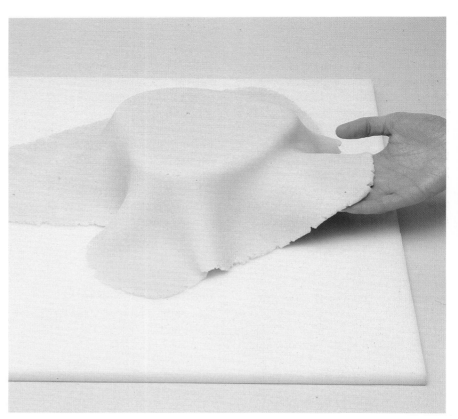

Carefully drape the marzipan over the cake, lifting the edges slightly to help it fall without breaking.

Carefully remove greaseproof paper, taking care not to damage the corners. Turn cake upsidedown to provide a good flat surface and stick on a board with a little softened marzipan. If the edges of the cake do not sit level on the cake board, make a sausage of marzipan and push into the gaps with a palette knife. Fill any visible holes and repair damaged corners with marzipan. Smooth over the cake.

To apply, lift up the left side of the marzipan and lay it over the rolling pin or your right arm. Lift the pin or your arm and drape the bottom of the marzipan against the side of the cake; the right side of the marzipan should still be on the board. Drape over the top of the cake, transfer marzipan to the left hand and support it while you remove air bubbles by brushing your right hand across the top of the cake.

Skirt out the corners and, using the flat of your hand, smooth the marzipan to the sides of the cake with an upward movement. If a downward movement is used, it drags the marzipan and weakens the paste at the corners and edges. Use smoothers to eliminate any finger marks and bumps. Smooth the corners and upper edge using your warm hands. Place the flat edge of a knife against the cake at the base, then cut away excess.

After smoothing the marzipan, cut off the surplus marzipan level with the bottom of the cake.

Marzipanning a Cake for Royal Icing

For a royal iced cake the marzipan is applied in two stages. First the cake top is coated, then the sides. For the sides of a square cake, the marzipan is best applied using four rectangles.

Working with marzipan.
Marzipan is an easy medium to work with, and the same basic rules apply to all marzipan work. As in all sugarcraft, hygiene is important.

Be sure that all work surfaces are clean and free from any dust or grease. Some of the new plastic non-stick boards and rolling pins make the work much easier. All equipment should be thoroughly cleaned as well. Always wash hands and clean fingernails before beginning work. Some cake decorators wear thin plastic surgical gloves to ensure cleanliness.

Measure the sides of the cake. Cut a strip of greaseproof paper the depth of the cake and long enough to go all around (or measure with string). Roll the marzipan and cut to size. Spread with boiled apricot purée, then roll the cake onto it.

Spread boiled apricot jam purée over the top of the cake. Roll out a round of marzipan to the size of the cake on a little icing sugar.
Place the cake on the marzipan and press well down to make sure there is a good seal. Trim away any excess marzipan.

Take care not to overlap where the paste meets. Place the cake on a board at least 5cm (2in) larger than the cake.

Applying Sugarpaste

The cake does not need to be covered with marzipan first. It can, if preferred, be covered in two layers of sugarpaste instead. The first layer is usually thinner and should be allowed to skin and harden before adding the final layer. Both layers are applied in the same way.

Knead the sugarpaste as for marzipan, kneading in colour if using.

Roll out the sugarpaste on a light dusting of icing sugar. Too much sugar will dry the paste and make it crack. Use the spacers to keep the thickness of the paste uniform. Measure the cake as for marzipan and roll out the sugarpaste a little larger all round.

Before applying the paste, sterilize the surface of the cake by wiping the marzipan with clear spirit such as gin, vodka or kirsch. Using the palm of your hand or a brush, make sure the entire surface is moist. If there are any dry patches, the paste may not stick to the marzipan and an air bubble could result.

Drape sugarpaste over cake.

Lift and drape the paste over the cake using the same technique as for marzipan. Skirt out the corners and smooth out any creases using an upward movement. Remember that rings or long fingernails could mark the surface. Use smoothers to rub over the top and sides of the cake and to round the corners.

If any air bubbles have been trapped under the paste, insert a clean needle into the bubble at an angle. Smooth over with your hand to expel the air and rub with a smoother. If the pin hole is still visible, this can be easily hidden with a small dot of icing of the same colour piped into the hole and then wiped away to leave a smooth finish.

Using a cranked palette knife, trim excess paste away carefully and smooth over cut area.

Smooth and cut at base.

Using your hand rub the top of the cake until it feels like silk and round edge in the same way.

Wipe away any sugar on the board and store the cake in a dry place until the sugarpaste has skinned and you are ready to decorate it. The ideal container is a cardboard box.

Sugarpaste

    15g (½oz) gelatine
    50ml (2fl oz/¼ cup) cold water
    25g (¾oz) glycerine
    125ml (4fl oz/½ cup) liquid
    glucose
    900g (2lb/8 cups) icing
    (confectioner's) sugar, sifted

Soak the gelatine in the cold water and place over hot water until dissolved and clear. (Do not allow the gelatine to boil.)

Add the glycerine and glucose to the gelatine. Stir until melted. Add the mixture to the icing sugar. Knead to a soft consistency.

Colouring sugarpaste

Adding colour to sugarpaste is better done in natural light, as artificial light can affect colour perception.

Add a little at a time; more can always be added later. If the colour is too dark, add another piece of paste and knead again. A pale base colour generally looks more pleasing and nicely sets off the colours of the flowers, ribbons, and other decorations.

To colour a large amount of paste, divide into small pieces, colour each one, then knead all the pieces together to blend.

After kneading in the colour, cut the paste in half to see if streaks are visible. If so, re-knead and cut again until all streaking has disappeared.

Marbling

Streaks can however be used to create a marbled effect. To achieve this, colour is kneaded into the paste slightly. When the paste is rolled out, the surface has a definite streaky pattern.

Making Royal Icing

Royal Icing

2 large or 3 medium egg whites
approximately 450g (1lb/4 cups)
icing (confectioner's) sugar

Use eggs at room temperature. Break
the white carefully into a clean bowl
and leave to liquify. Make sure no
yolk gets into the egg white as this will
make the icing heavy and yellow.

The icing sugar should be fresh,
dry and free of lumps. If there are
lumps, put it through a spotlessly
clean sieve.

Add 5ml (1tsp) glycerine at room
temperature when icing has reached
full peak to prevent it from setting
too hard. Add it just before use. For
softer icing use more glycerine.

Note: Glycerine must not be used
when making piped flowers, runouts
or lace as they will not set hard
enough.

Mixing by hand

All utensils for making royal icing
must be spotlessly clean.
Place egg whites in a clean bowl.
Beat half of the icing sugar in well,
then add the rest a little at a time
until full peak is reached. Scrape the
sides of the bowl down well with a
plastic scraper. Beat by hand for
about ten minutes. By this time the
icing should be light and fluffy and
able to hold its shape.
Store at room temperature in an
airtight plastic container.

Electric mixer method

If making royal icing with an electric
mixer, set at the slowest speed and
use a beater. Work as for hand
mixing, beating for a few seconds
each time a little sugar is added. It
should take about four minutes
all together. Scrape the sides of the
bowl frequently with the plastic
scraper.

Using powdered egg white

Royal icing made from powdered
egg white is whiter and easier to
work with as it sets quickly and
hard. Use 15ml (3tsp) powdered
egg white and 75ml (2½fl oz/⅓
cup) cold water to 450g (1lb/4
cups) icing sugar. Stir the powder
into the water, then make the icing
by either of the methods described.
Add a little extra sugar or egg white
if necessary to achieve the right
consistency.

Colouring royal icing

Icing can be coloured with liquid or
paste food colours, but paste colours
are preferable because they give a
dense colour without altering the
consistency of the icing.

When colouring a small amount
of icing for piping, put the icing on
a side scraper. Add colour and use
a palette knife to blend in the colour
with a backwards and forwards
motion. If colouring a large amount
of icing, colour some on a scaper
first, then incorporate this into the
bowl of icing.

Liquid colours are useful if a
colour is to be repeated. Use an
eyedropper to add the colour until
the desired shade is reached, then
record how many drops were added
to the amount of icing.

Choosing Colours

The overall appearance of a cake is
greatly enhanced by the correct use
of colour. Therefore a basic
knowledge of the colour spectrum
and the way in which colours
complement each other is useful.

The spectrum is the range of
colours as seen in a rainbow; by
mixing these basic colours an infinite
range of shades is obtained.

There are three colour schemes to
use – monochrome, contrasting or
complementary and harmonious.
Monochrome is the easiest as only
shades of one colour are used.
Contrasting or complementary colours
are opposite each other on the spectrum. Harmony colours are three
to six colours being used which are
next to each other on the spectrum.

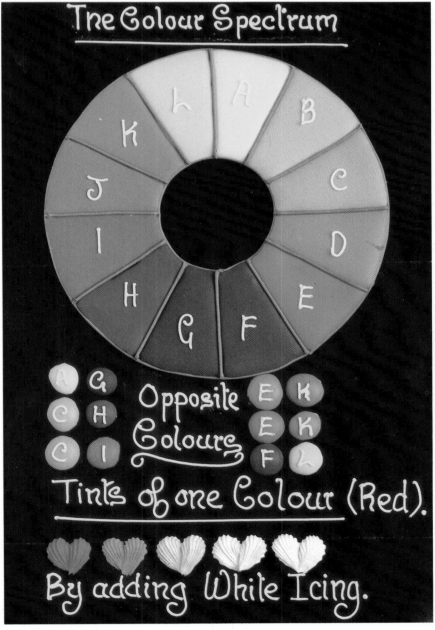

The Colour Spectrum

Opposite Colours

Tints of one Colour (Red).

By adding White Icing.

Applying Royal Icing

It is essential to get a smooth flat iced surface, so be sure the marzipan has been properly applied.

Prepare the royal icing. Colour may be added just before icing. Put the paste in gradually using a cocktail stick or similar to obtain the desired shade. Keep the icing in the bowl covered with a damp cloth at all times to prevent crusting.

Place the cake on a turntable. Using a palette knife put icing on the top. With the knife, spread the icing over the cake, working with a paddle movement to eliminate bubbles. At the same time slowly rotate the turntable with the other hand. When the icing is evenly spread take the cake off the turntable and place on a worktop.

Place a metal straight edge at the edge of the cake away from you at an angle of about 45° to the surface. Draw it across the cake in one continuous movement. Move the straight edge backwards and forwards across the cake until the top is flat.

Remove any icing from the side of the cake and leave the cake to dry in a warm place.

When the top is dry, ice the sides. Put the cake on the turntable. Spread the icing around the sides working from bottom to top with a paddling motion. Slowly rotate the turntable at the same time. Hold the scraper towards you at an angle of about 15° against the side of the cake. With the other hand, slowly rotate the turntable in one continuous movement all the way round then pull the scraper off towards yourself.

A takeoff mark will be left which can be scraped down with a knife when dry.

Give the cake two to four coats of icing, drying and smoothing completely between each. Remove any loose icing before adding another coat. Coat the cake board each time, if preferred.

A softer royal icing can be used for the final coat if wished. Leave the cake to dry thoroughly before decorating.

If a scroll or shell border is to be used, the top and sides may be iced at the same time. For runout borders or small shells a sharp edge is needed so ice the sides at least eight hours after the top.

Using a Piping Bag

The bag when filled will fit comfortably into one hand. The other is then left free to steady it.

Hold the bag as you would hold a short, very fat pencil, with the thumb and index finger either side and the third finger bent underneath. The fourth and fifth fingers are also bent under. The folded end of the bag will then fit snugly into the hand between the thumb and index finger.

For smaller amounts of icing the bag will not reach as far as the palm, so hold it with the thumb and first two fingers. Always make sure the thumb is on the folded end, keeping the bag firmly closed.

If this position seems uncomfortable at first, persevere, as it enables the most pressure to be applied with the least effort. This is very important if you are piping for a long time.

Pressure is applied by the thumb and first two fingers which are in contact with the bag. Fine movement is also achieved by use of these fingers.

Do not hold the bag with both hands as this restricts movement and control. If two hands are necessary to force the icing through the tube, then it is too stiff or has been made incorrectly.

To make a piping bag, measure and cut a piece of greaseproof paper twice as long as it is wide. Fold the paper diagonally. (The points will not meet.) Cut along the fold with a sharp knife, making two right-angle triangles. Lay the triangle flat with the right angle facing you, then fold the corner inwards.

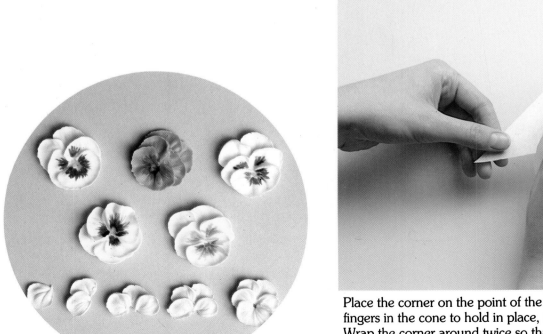

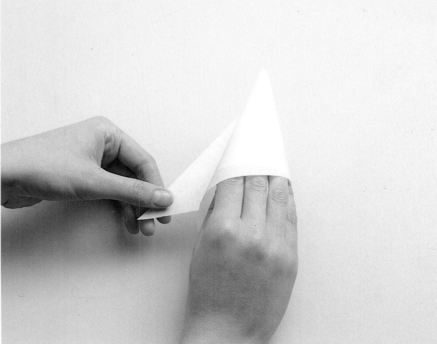

Place the corner on the point of the right angle to make a cone. Put your fingers in the cone to hold in place, then bring the other corner over it. Wrap the corner around twice so that the points meet. Slide the three points together to tighten the bag. Fold the top point into the bag. If a tube is being used, first cut off the tip of the bag with scissors, insert the tube and fill with icing.

SIMPLE DECORATIONS

There are many spectacular decorations to be achieved quite simply. Crimping, embossing and ribbon insertion look most impressive, with the Garrett frill making very pretty cake designs. Cutwork also produces excellent finishes.

Heart cake: *A cream sugarpasted heart cake, suitable for a small wedding, decorated with crimper work and topped with a sugar orchid. A variety of other sugar flowers may be used (see pages 144-145).*

Crimping

Crimpers are stainless steel tools used to impress and pinch a design onto soft freshly applied sugarpaste. It is a technique that beginners can easily master to produce a professional finish, and it is an ideal way of disguising marks on a poorly finished cake. Practise beforehand on a spare piece of sugarpaste.

Crimping can be done on any part of the cake but is most effective used on the top edge or the sides. Use crimper work sparingly, or the cake will look cluttered.

Crimpers are available in nine different designs: oval, curve, scallop, double scallop, diamond, vee, straight line, heart and holly.

To ensure adequate control of the crimpers, twist an elastic band around the head of the tool, positioned a quarter of the way down the arms. This makes sure the crimpers do not spring open when in use and tear the paste.

Mark the position of the pattern on the cake by using a paper template attached to the sides of the cake, or mark out the design using pin pricks.

Dip the serrated end of the crimper into cornflour occasionally so that it does not stick to the paste. Insert crimpers into the sugarpaste and pinch together, release slowly and withdraw the crimpers. It is important to release the crimpers slowly and remove carefully each time, as the paste can easily be torn or pulled too far from the cake, making the pattern irregular. Crimp the pattern around the cake.

Crimping can be used as a border around the base of a cake. Simply roll a thin strip of paste, long enough to go around the cake. Cut the ends at an angle, place round the cake and butt the ends together. Then crimp the border.

Crimping can also be used on marzipan.

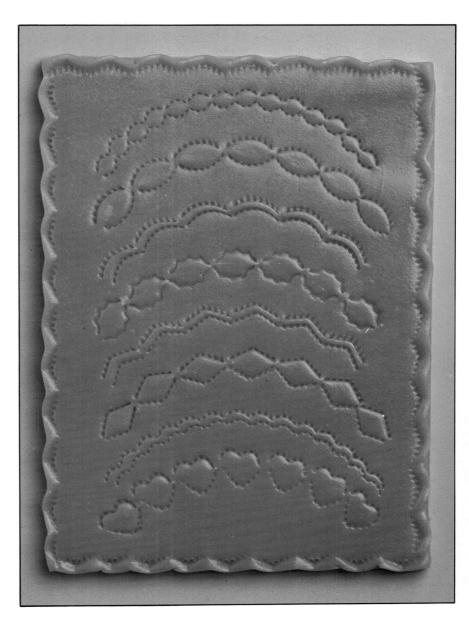

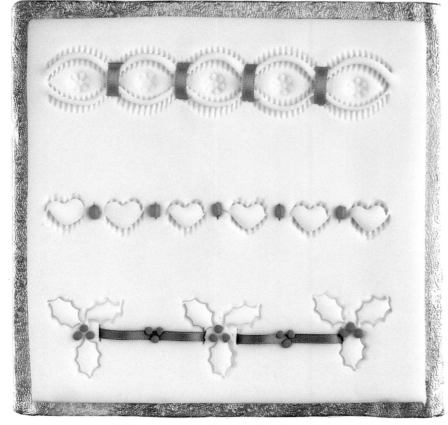

Crimper work and ribbon insertion (see overleaf).

Crimpers and designs made with crimpers on marzipan.

Embossing

Similar to crimper work, embossing must also be worked on fresh sugarpaste. Crimping and embossing can be used together producing imaginative results.

Many tools can be used to impress a pattern into the sugarpaste. Available from craft shops, various leather embossing tools are very effective. Decorative spoon handles can produce interesting effects. To add delicate finishes to small scallops and flowers, use the tops of piping tubes.

Embossing can be used on the cake board as well as the cake. It also looks effective as an edging around a plaque.

Both crimper work and embossing look effective combined with embroidery, lace and ribbon insertion. Brushing with edible dusting powder or painting with food colouring can provide areas of colour.

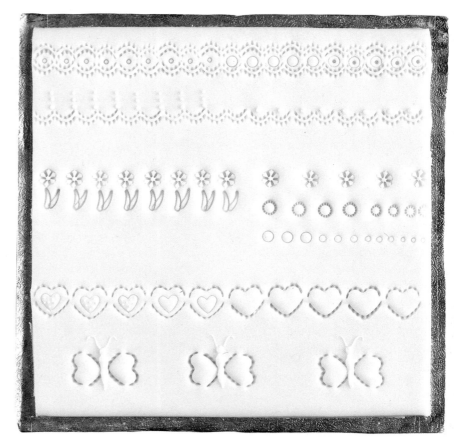

Above: Embossing with piping tubes combined with crimper designs.

Crimper work and embossing used together.

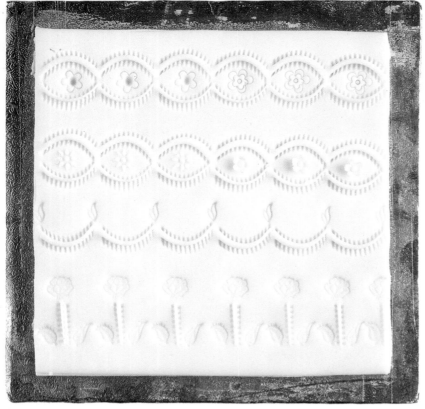

Below: Crimper work designs for Christmas cakes.

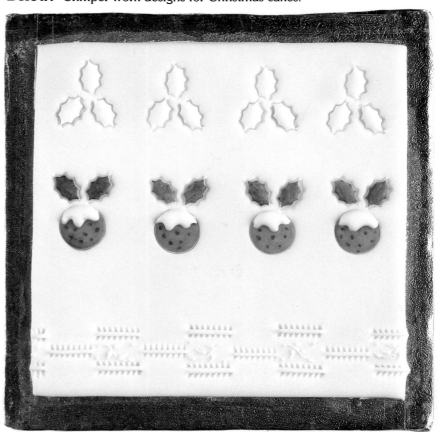

Ribbon Insertion and Banding

Ribbon insertion creates the illusion that ribbon has been threaded through the sugarpaste. Ribbon banding is a way of using bands of ribbon to finish off a cake.

Choose coloured ribbons that pick out any coloured icing for stunning effects.

Ribbon insertion can only be applied to soft sugarpaste. First measure and mark the section with a scriber so that the lines are straight and an equal distance apart. Make a slit in the paste using a scalpel or ribbon insertion tool. If using narrow ribbon, fold a piece of ribbon about 1cm (⅜in) long in half and place in the slit with tweezers.

For wider ribbon, cut the ribbon slightly longer than the space between slits. The ribbon should be long enough to make a loop instead of lying flat. Make the loops equal.

Moisten the ribbon ends with a little egg white and then place one edge in each slit using tweezers.

For ribbon banding, apply to the sugarpaste when dry. Adhere to the cake with dots of icing. Hide the join with a small bow.

Both ribbon insertion and banding look effective with other techniques such as crimping, embroidery, broderie anglaise and lace work. Lace pieces can be applied between ribbon inserts or on the ribbon edges. Pipe embroidery onto the ribbon, particulary banding, or onto the cake to give an appearance of holding the ribbon in place.

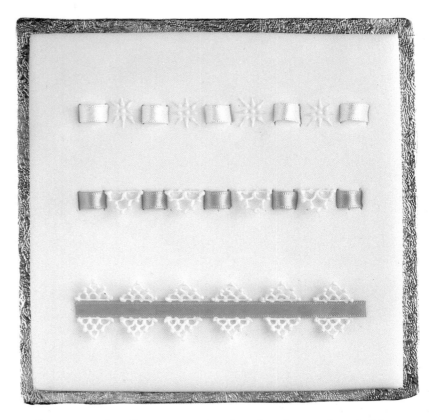

Crimper work, ribbon insertion, embroidery, lacework and ribbon banding.

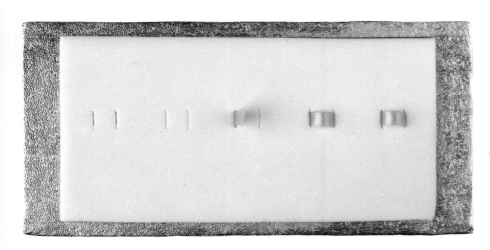

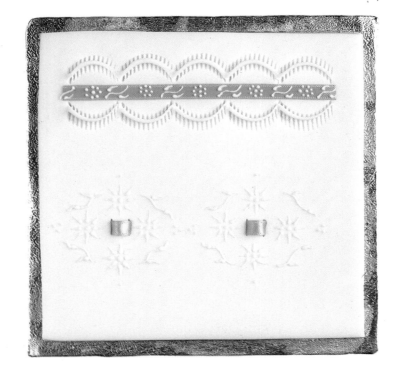

Wedding Bells

The frilled and embroidered bells could be displayed as shown, or placed on a perspex cake stand. Bake the cakes in bell shaped tin and cover with white sugarpaste. Add frills, sugar or artificial flowers, piping and broderie anglaise as shown.

Garrett Frill

One of the prettiest cake decorations, the Garrett frill is surprisingly easy to do. Named after Elaine Garrett, who introduced the idea, these delicate frills are made using special frill cutters.

To enable the frill to keep its lift, first knead 5ml (1tsp) gum tragacanth into 450g (1lb) sugarpaste. Leave for at least 24 hours.

Frills are best applied to a deep sided sugarpasted cake which has dried for a few days. Pipe a snailstrail around the cake base, as where the frilling flounces it will show the base.

Scribe a line on the cake side where the frill is to sit. Thinly roll out the paste and cut out a circle with the cutter. Remove a centre circle – the size of this determines the depth of the frill. Make a cut in the circle and open out the frill.

Move the frill near the edge of the board. Put a cocktail stick halfway up the paste and, putting an index finger on top of the stick, rotate it. As the stick moves forward over the paste it will make a frill. Repeat along the edge of the paste.

Brush a thin line of water along the scribed line. Gently attach the frill. Lift the frill in places using a paintbrush.

When applying more than one frill, work from the base upwards. Overlap each frill by half the depth of the previous one.

There are many ways to finish the upper edge of the frill. Try piping a snailstrail, flowers or dots. Lace pieces or flowers may be attached.

For a more definite lift to the frill, use a flouncing or anger tool rotated gently in the same way on the edge of the paste.

If using petal dusting powder, brush onto the cut out paste before frilling. When colouring layers of frills, make each frill a paler shade than the last one, the darkest colour at the base.

Double frill

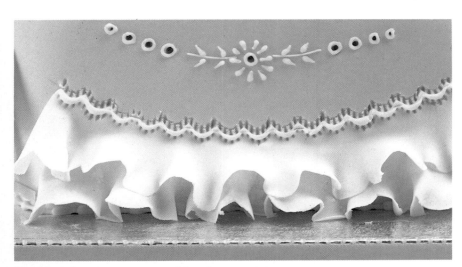

Double frill with crimping and broderie anglaise.

Triple frill

Broderie Anglaise

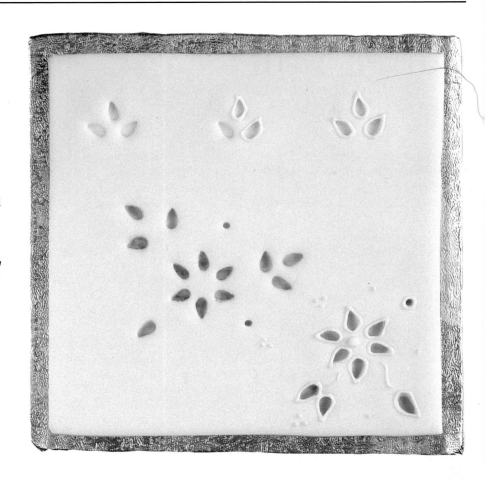

Broderie anglaise is a delicate technique so take care at the piping stage. Various tools may be used to indent the soft sugarpaste. Use the pointed end of a knitting needle or the rounded end of a paintbrush to obtain the correct size hole. The leaf or petal shape can be made by pinching a writing tube (No 8 or smaller) into the correct shape with a pair of pliers. Fill the end of the tube with modelling paste and let dry.

Make the pattern holes in the sugarpaste and leave to skin. Pipe round the edges of the indentations with a fine tube. The broderie anglaise can be coloured either by painting inside the indented shapes

or using a little edible dusting powder. Take care to apply the colour so that it does not mark the surface of the cake. Another method would be to use coloured icing for piping. Whatever the method, keep to pastel shades.

Ideas for patterns can be found by looking at broderie anglaise fabric or trim. To give the raised satin stitch effect seen on some cloth, use soft peak royal icing. Pipe quite a lot on the edge of the flower and brush towards the centre with a fine damp sable brush so that it has that heavy rounded satiny appearance.

These plaques show different styles of broderie anglaise.

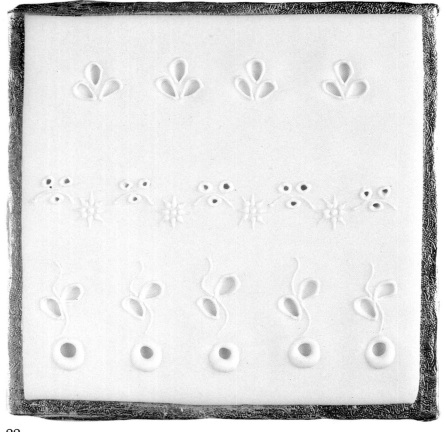

Broderie Anglaise Plaque

Trace the design and transfer to the prepared plaque, which must be soft enough to insert a tool to make the holes. Pipe the design using a fine tube. The icing can be white, as shown, or coloured.

Template

Finished plaque

Painting on Sugarpaste

Beginners often use conventional colour schemes. By experimentation and trial and error a good sense of colour should develop and more creative designs should be possible.

Avoid the temptation to use colour straight from the container as few of these basic colours are true to nature. Experiment with colour by mixing.

Harmonious colours are used to give a balanced appearance to a cake. Colours from opposite sides of the colour wheel can be used together to create a striking effect, as long as one of the colours is used for detail only.

It is possible to paint directly onto the surface of completely dry sugarpaste. Use paste or liquid food colour. If painting for the first time do not paint directly onto the cake's surface as it is difficult to remove

mistakes. Instead paint onto a plaque which can be placed on a cake if wished.

When applying colour to sugarpaste, keep the brush fairly dry. Too much moisture will cause streaking and may affect the surface of the paste.

If painting a scene, subtle blending of colour can be achieved by brushing one colour into the next while both are still wet.

If a pattern or quilt with clear defined lines is to be painted, one colour should be completely dry before an adjacent colour or surface pattern is applied.

If you plan to duplicate a favourite cake, make a note of how a certain colour has been achieved. This applies to painting onto paste as well as mixing colour into paste.

Cat Cake

Paint the cat directly on the surface of the cake, then frame the painting with moulded flowers and grass.
Mark the position of the cat. Do not mark out the other details as these are painted freehand. The background tones are quite muted and the colours become stronger towards the foreground. The flowers and leaves are moulded and positioned last to complete the three-dimensional effect.

Fox Cub Cake

The cocoa-painting fox cub plaque can be removed and saved as a souvenir of the occasion.

Coat cake and board with marbled beige and brown coloured sugarpaste. (For marbling, *see* page 12.) Add ribbon banding as shown. Make the fox cub plaque opposite. Attach to cake with royal icing.

Cocoa Painting

tones. In the fourth pot make a dark concentrated mixture to define eyes and shadows. While painting, re-heat the water if the mixtures become too stiff. If you must leave the design before its completion simply cover the pots and store. To use again, place the pots in hot water and stir well, as the cocoa colour tends to separate.

Start by covering the image and surrounding background in the palest tone.

Next paint in the medium tone.

Proceed to more clearly defined areas using the darkest of the three tones. Leave the plaque to dry. Apply the final very dark concentrated colour to the pupils of the eyes, whiskers, deepest shadows, etc.

When the necessary colour has been added and the plaque is dry, use a scalpel to scratch away some of the cocoa colour from eyes or other small areas to give highlights. Mark the fur in the direction it grows. Scratch away finer details such as corn and grass.

Cocoa painting, a method similar to painting in oils, is an easy way to decorate a cake. The design can be painted directly onto the surface of the cake, or onto a sugarpaste, gelatine or marzipan plaque. The latter method enables the painting to be kept as a souvenir of the occasion, as the plaque can be removed before the cake is cut.

It is best to tint the plaque a shade of cream, as this colour blends nicely with brown. Beginners could start by copying a card or picture whose design is printed in sepia (brown) tones.

The design should not be drawn in detail, just the features and a rough outline. Too many lines will spoil the finished result as they tend to show through the cocoa where the tones are light.

Cocoa butter can be used but this is difficult to find and expensive. Coconut oil produces the same effect and is easily available from health food shops.

If you don't wish to paint freehand, you can easily trace a picture onto the plaque. First trace the design onto tracing paper. Turn the tracing paper over and retrace the image on the back using a brown lip pencil.

Place the paper on the plaque, right sides uppermost. Using a scribe or similar pointed tool, retrace the lines. The design should then be visible on the plaque.

Put a teaspoon of coconut oil into each of four containers. Place the containers into a shallow pan of hot water, then add a little cocoa to the first container, a little more to the second and even more to the third. You should have three distinct

Cocoa Paintings

Baby owl

Country village scene

Puppies

Persian cat

Painting on Plaques

Plaques are convenient when decorating a cake in a hurry as they can be prepared in advance. As long as they are stored correctly, preferably in a cardboard box in a dry place, they will last indefinitely. A plaque mounted on a velvet covered cake board or a wooden base would be a unique gift. Choose a design that can be used for a number of different occasions. A message suitable for the event can be piped on when the plaque is to be used.

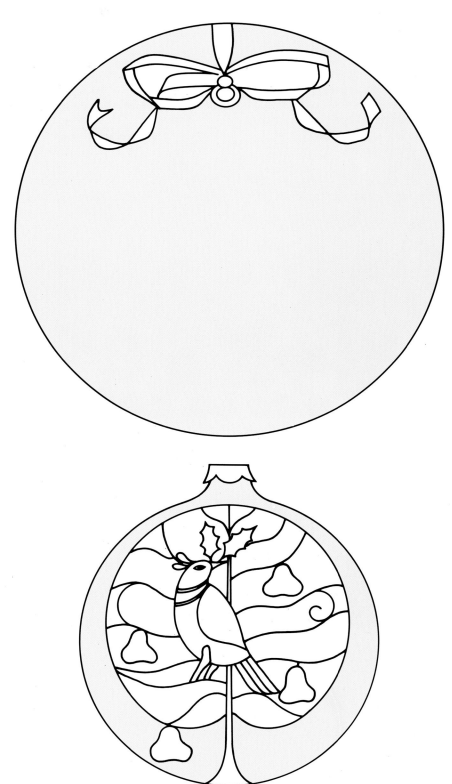

Partridge in a pear tree

The black lines have been made with a food pen. Paste colours have been used for the tree and bird and non-toxic gold for the pears.

Cutwork

Cutwork is a technique in which biscuit, aspic and flower cutters are used to create simple sugarpaste and marzipan shapes. More original and intricate designs can be achieved if cardboard templates are used.

If using templates make them out of fine card, such as the sides of cereal boxes, as this is durable and has a firm edge against which to place the scalpel when cutting. This will give a clean, sharp edge to the paste or marzipan which is most important in cutwork. Use a sharp craft knife or scalpel. Nothing will spoil the overall effect more than indistinct shapes or damaged lines.

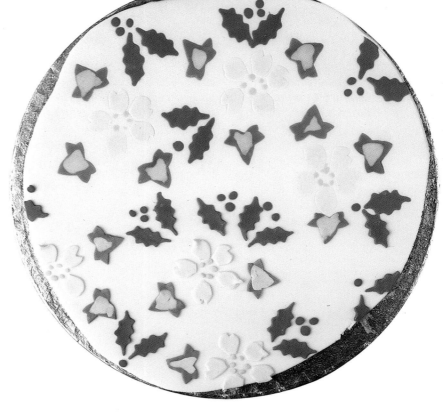

Above: Marzipan Christmas cutwork
Below: Sugarpaste Father Christmas cutwork

Template for lettering

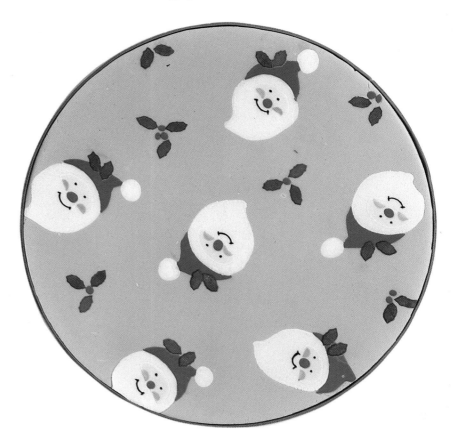

Templates for Father Christmas pieces

Cutwork Christmas Tree

Cut out the sugarpaste Christmas
tree and pot. Make small templates
and cut out enough shapes to fully
decorate tree.

Finished plaque

Template

Cutwork Clown

Make cardboard templates for all pattern shapes. Start painting the background and work forward. Keep the colours fresh and bright. Add finishing touches by painting in clothes, shoes, etc. Remember that the brush colours will not be true when applied to coloured paste. For example yellow paint will become green if put on blue paste. Therefore if a lot of the pattern is to be painted on, it is better to cut out the shapes in white sugarpaste.

Finished plaque

Template

Christmas Parcel Cake

The Christmas parcel is wrapped with a sheet of cutwork sugarpaste and tied with a big red ribbon bow. Cut out coloured shapes in sugarpaste. Roll out more sugarpaste to cover the cake. Place the cutouts on the sugarpaste before it starts to skin. Place a piece of waxed or greaseproof paper over the cutouts, then roll over the area *once* quite firmly. Remove the paper and cover the cake in the usual way.

Marzipan Cutwork Christmas Decorations

These decorations are very simple to make and do not need templates. The bodies are equilateral triangles, and the arms are smaller triangles. The other pieces are all based on sections cut from circles.

Trace the photograph and make cardboard templates. Roll out yellow marzipan and cut the two pieces for the body. Mark the lines with the back of a knife and make indentations for the buttons. The hair is a tapered sausage turned up at the ends.

Use a fluted round cutter for the wings. Cut out a triangle and mark with a knife. For the halo, make a ring and flatten slightly.

Cut a circle of pink marzipan for the head. Mark the eyes with a half-moon tool. The nose is a pink ball. Position another pink ball for the mouth, insert a cocktail stick, and rock up and down. Cut a smaller pink circle for the hands, cut in half, then cut out a small triangle to represent the fingers and thumb. Assemble the angel on a thin cake board or on top of a cake.

For the Father Christmas, cut a red, pink and white circle using the same round cutter. Cut sections from the circles as shown for the hat, face and beard.

Marzipan Inlay Designs

Inlay Bee

Roll out blue marzipan and cut to fit a thin cake board. Use a fish-shaped biscuit cutter or draw a template to cut out the fish from the plaque. For the fish, colour equal strips of marzipan. Lay the strips side by side and roll out. Cut out the fish shapes and carefully place in the plaque. Roll over gently with a rolling pin, and mark with a grater. The cutout fish have inlay stripes in contrasting colours.

This design is based on circles. Use round cutters to cut the body and head from yellow marzipan. Roll out black marzipan and cut a circle using the same cutters as for the body.

Cut two strips and position on the body. Trim and go over gently with a rolling pin to fix to the body. Cut small black circles for eyes.

Cut a white circle, then cut in half and shape for the wings. Assemble the bee as shown and trim with marzipan.
Position on a thin cake board or place on top of a cake.

ROYAL ICING WORK

Concentrating on basic piping skills produces attractive finished cakes. Once perfected, move on to the delicate beauty of embroidery and broderie anglaise. Lettering is another cake adornment to master.

Anemone cake: *A beautifully delicate cake for a birthday or special occasion.*

Cover a round cake with cream sugarpaste. Create the brush embroidery following the template opposite. Pipe the tassel border in cream and overpipe in colours to match the embroidery.

Brush Embroidery

This embroidery can be done with soft royal icing but you must work quickly to finish before it dries. Adding about 5ml (1tsp) piping gel to a cup of icing slows down the drying and gives a smoother surface. Use a No 1 tube for all embroidery, increasing the pressure where more icing is needed. Always start with the part of the design which appears to be the furthest away, to give depth to the finished work. (For further details of basic and tube embroidery, see pages 42-45.)

Pipe the outline, working on a small area at a time. Flood just inside the line. Brush the icing down towards the centre of the flower with a small, flat brush which is slightly damp. Continue with each petal, finishing with the one nearest you.

If you use care, it is not necessary to pipe the outlines first. Pipe the line but increase the pressure at the outer edge where you would usually flood it. Always work down towards the point where the petal or leaf is attached to the plant.

When the brush work is completely dry, pipe in any detail, such as stamens in flowers or veins in leaves, using a fine tube. Place the finished plaque in the centre of a plain iced cake.

Template for the brush embroidery plaque shown here.

Basic Piping

Writing tubes

To pipe a straight line, work towards your body. Touch the tube to the cake surface and apply light, even pressure, pulling away immediately to avoid making a bulb at the beginning of the line. Lift the tube up and about 3cm (1½in) away from the surface. Keep your eye on the line to be followed. When about 4cm (1½in) from the end of the line, stop the pressure and gently lower the tube into position. With practice you will be able to finish the piped line in exactly the right place.

When piping a line with angles, such as a zigzag, touch the tube to the surface of the cake each time you change direction.

Star and shell tubes

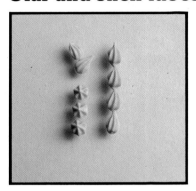

No 6 star tube.

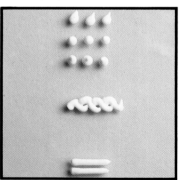

No 4 writing tube.

No 15 star tube.

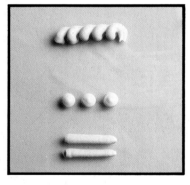

No 3 writing tube.

No 9 star tube.

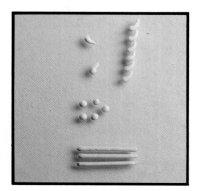

No 2 writing tube.

No 12 star tube.

No 42 shell tube.

No 44 shell tube.

No 5 shell tube.

No 7 star tube.

No 8 star tube.

Petal and basket weave tubes

No 56 flower or petal tube.

No 59 flower or petal tube.

No 23 basket weave tube.

Pressure Piping—Birds

Pressure piping is a technique of increasing and decreasing piping pressure to make three-dimensional effects. Animals, birds and figures to bows, hearts and bootees can all be pressure piped. To start piping, decide which area should appear furthest away and pipe that part first, then gradually build up the complete subject, increasing the pressure where necessary.

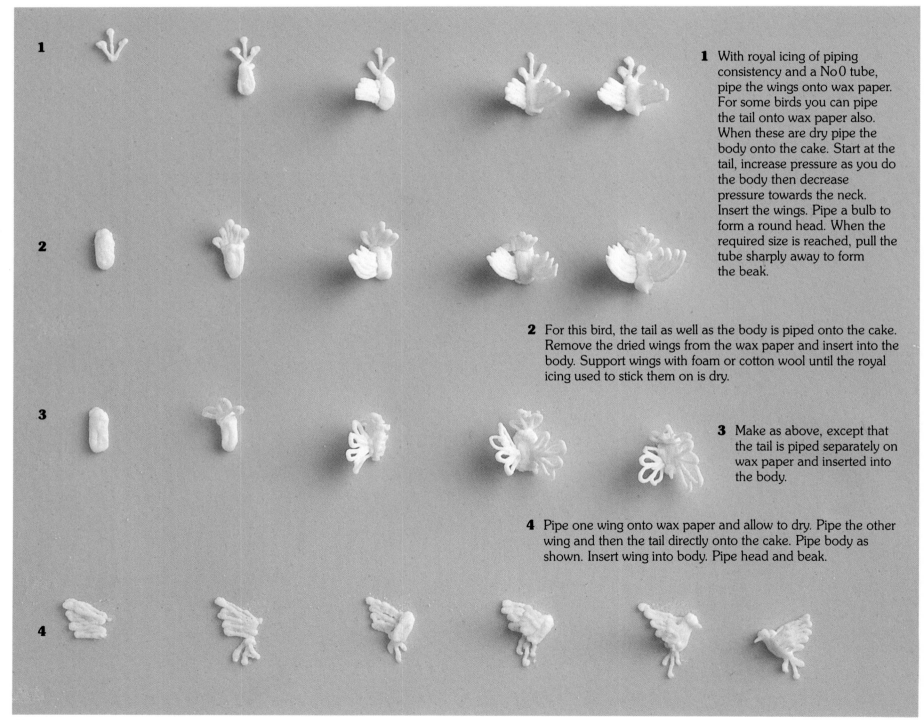

1 With royal icing of piping consistency and a No 0 tube, pipe the wings onto wax paper. For some birds you can pipe the tail onto wax paper also. When these are dry pipe the body onto the cake. Start at the tail, increase pressure as you do the body then decrease pressure towards the neck. Insert the wings. Pipe a bulb to form a round head. When the required size is reached, pull the tube sharply away to form the beak.

2 For this bird, the tail as well as the body is piped onto the cake. Remove the dried wings from the wax paper and insert into the body. Support wings with foam or cotton wool until the royal icing used to stick them on is dry.

3 Make as above, except that the tail is piped separately on wax paper and inserted into the body.

4 Pipe one wing onto wax paper and allow to dry. Pipe the other wing and then the tail directly onto the cake. Pipe body as shown. Insert wing into body. Pipe head and beak.

Piping Shapes over a Mould

Many objects are suitable for this work, and there are many commercial moulds available. If fine work is to be done, the article must be fairly small. The design must be piped freehand.

To make the bells, first draw around the base of the bell. Divide this circle into equal sections. Grease the outside of the mould with white fat. Place the mould on the pattern as a guide for the vertical lines. Pipe the lines from top to bottom, dividing the bell into equal sections. Fill in the spaces with an S-design or freehand flowers or, if the lines are closer together, dots. Make sure the lines touch each other. Leave to dry. When dry, warm the shape slightly to melt the fat and release the filigree shape.

Basic Embroidery

Piped embroidery is a series of straight and curved lines, dots, leaf and flower shapes etc, put together in a design.

When doing embroidery on the side of a cake it is much easier if you tilt it away from yourself; a cake tilter is a useful piece of equipment.

Lily of the valley: For all methods, pipe a stem first. Pipe oval bulbs of icing. Clean the end of the tube, insert into the centre of the bulb and pull downwards sharply. Buds are graduated oval bulbs.

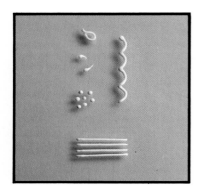

Dots: Piped dots should not have points so keep the icing soft. Just touch the tube to the cake surface, apply pressure and stop when the dot is the required size.

Pulled dots: Pipe dot then pull the tube away to the side.

Leaf shape: Start at the point, curve around and finish neatly. The sides can be curved slightly or more deeply as in a teardrop.

Flowers: These can be five dots piped around one dot; pulled dots around one dot; or leaf shapes piped in a circle, pointing in or out.

Pipe an oval bulb with three piped dots beneath.

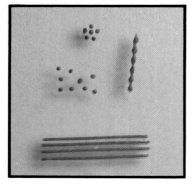

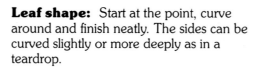

Think of an elephant! Pipe one 'ear' – a pulled curved dot. Pipe the second 'ear' – a reversed curved pulled dot. Then pipe the 'trunk' – squeezed in between the 'ears'. Press towards the cake and then sharply out again.

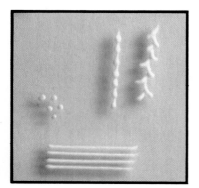

Snowdrops: Pipe three teardrops with a bulb at the top.

Tube Embroidery

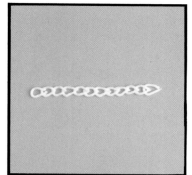

Chainstitch: Pipe an open teardrop. Pipe a second open teardrop starting inside the open end of the first.

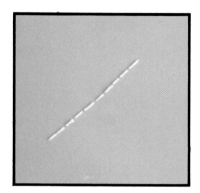

Back stitch: As for running stitch but leave much smaller gaps between 'stitches'.

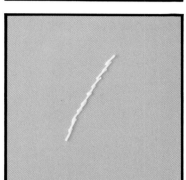

Stem stitch: Pipe short strokes in a line, each stroke overlapping the preceding one slightly.

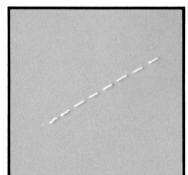

Running stitch: Pipe short lines at even intervals.

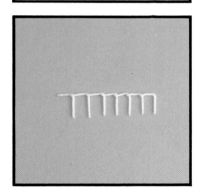

Buttonhole: Pipe a line from left to right then down at a right angle. The second stitch starts inside the corner of the first.

Herringbone: Pipe a diagonal line going down from right to left. Pipe a second diagonal line in the opposite direction which crosses the first towards the bottom of the 'stitch'. The third line crosses the second towards the top.

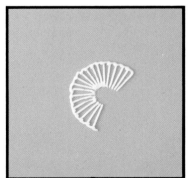

Buttonhole wheel: As for buttonhole but the lines are piped to form a circle. Take care that the right angled lines all point towards the centre.

Cross-stitch: Pipe two lines of equal length crossing at the centre.

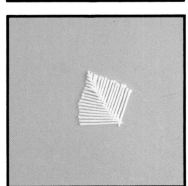

Fishbone stitch: This is useful for leaves with a central vein. Start at the outside edge of the leaf and pipe an angled line which just crosses the central vein. Pipe the second stitch from the opposite side to cross the vein from the opposite direction.

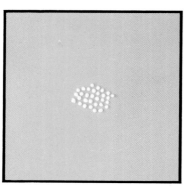

Seed stitch: Pipe very small dots close together. This is useful for flower centres.

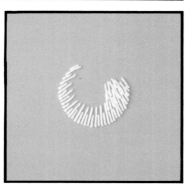

Long and short stitch: Pipe a row of long and short lines. The second row is piped to fill in the gaps.

Feather stitch: Pipe a small U-shaped line. Start the second stitch just above the centre of the first and pipe in the opposite direction.

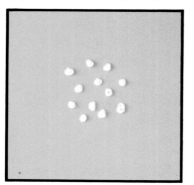

French knots: Pipe a small circle. Continue piping to fill in the centre and pull away in an untidy dot.

Lazy daisy: Pipe a series of leaf shapes to form a flower. Pipe small lines over the rounded ends.

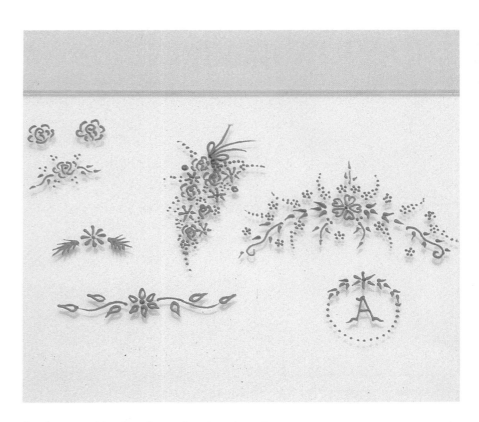

A selection of freehand piped embroidery designs, suitable for side decorations. Flower patterns can be done in a single colour, as shown, or in different coloured icing. For the initial in the circle, use letters from embroidery patterns or needlework books. (See also page 46.)

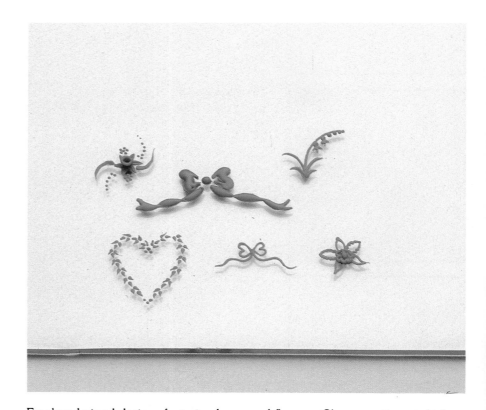

Freehand piped designs featuring bows and flowers. Choose patterns which complement the overall design of the cake. These patterns could also be used individually to decorate small cakes, petits fours or biscuits.

Tube Embroidery Plaque

Trace the design and transfer to a prepared rectangle plaque. Have ready several piping bags with fine tubes filled with the different colour icing. Pipe the design following the embroidery stitches. This kind of design can be adapted to use patterns from books on embroidery and other needlework.

Lettering

When attempting lettering it is important to take time to work out details such as layout, spacing and position on the cake or plaque.

Make sure the spacing of the letters looks even, and that the writing forms part of the overall design of the cake.

If words are written one below the other rather than along a line, it will make it easier to keep them looking straight. A scroll line can be piped below the words.

Although an experienced decorator will be able to pipe lettering directly onto a cake freehand, it is best to draw a plan of the cake top and experiment to find a suitable style, size and position for the letters.

The chosen lettering can then be traced and scratched onto the cake in the right place before piping.

Use icing to match the basecoat, as coloured icing will leave a stain if it is necessary to remove it. Over-piping can be done in a colour. Take off mistakes with a palette knife and try again.

Lettering can also be done with runouts (see page 49) on wax paper and then positioned on the cake with royal icing when dry. Ideal for numbers, initials and monograms.

Remember, practice, patience and a steady hand make perfect lettering.

The instructions for the Christmas cake can be found on page 151.

Plaques with Inscriptions

The plaques here are inscribed with various types of lettering. Prepare runout or sugarpaste plaques, then transfer the chosen lettering. Pipe the lettering. Finish off the plaque with piped flowers or other designs, or pressure pipe figures.

If wished, the plaque can be removed before the cake is cut and either saved as a momento or stored and used again.

ADVANCED ROYAL ICING

The most stunning effects can be achieved with royal icing. These more advanced aspects of sugar-craft include runout work, lace and filigree, intricate extension work, oriental stringwork and the most delicate tulle work.

Runout Christmas cake: This unusual Christmas cake features a side design of trees and a runout top decoration adapted from a Christmas card.

Coat the cake white on top. The sides are covered with a subtle blue-green sky and a few white clouds. White snow covers the bottom section, about 2.5 cm (1in) above board. Mottled coloured icing is put on the side and the scraper pulled around over it to make the sky. When dry snow and trees are piped freehand with No 0 and 1 with beige-grey royal icing. Pipe trees, fence etc as in a country landscape. Brush in snow with blue-grey wash on a No 3 sable brush. Pipe a bulb border with No 3 tube; red spots may be added.

Runout Work

Attractive runout work, or flood work, can be used to make a variety of cake decorations. The most popular are collars, but plaques, borders, figures, pictures, numbers and letters can all be made using the runout technique. The lace inserts and collars on pages 72-73 are excellent examples of this technique.

To make a runout

First select an outline, design or picture. Try a simple runout first, such as a shaped plaque. Place the chosen design under cellophane or roasting wrap pinned or stuck down onto a completely flat surface.

Make the runout icing. Add a little water to ordinary royal icing until a slow flowing consistency is achieved. Place the runout icing into a piping bag and cut a small hole in the tip to regulate the amount of icing flowing out and break any air bubbles in the icing.

First, outline the design using a fine writing tube. Next flood in the area with the runout icing. If necessary, use a fine paintbrush to ease the icing into difficult corners.

It is best to dry runouts in a warm place, preferably under a desk lamp with a flexible arm. Always make spare runouts in case of breakages.

Runout broderie anglaise collar.

For the two flower plaques make the runout backgrounds, dust with colour then pipe the stems for the flowers and the lilies of the valley. Position piped roses or forget-me-nots.

Runout Christmas Cake Plaque

Pipe an oval plaque and fill in. Leave to dry for four days. Work with No 0 tube and thick runout icing. Pipe the wheelbarrow first, doing the wheel last so that it stands out. When dry pipe mistletoe twigs all over. Use full peak beige-grey icing for the branches and pale green for the leaves. Pipe in the berries with No 0 tube and white royal icing. The mistletoe in the barrow is dusted with moss green dust.

Paint the girls in dark tones to give an old-fashioned look. Pipe the hair and scarf when dry and tone in with a damp sable brush. Dust flesh colour on the face and blend with a No 00 sable brush. Pipe the lace collar with a No 1 tube, then use a No 0 for the outside loops.

Templates for twigs.

Side designs pressure piped (see page 40) directly onto the cake.

Runout Christmas Cake Borders

Make the runout border. Outline with a No 1 tube. Outline and run out flower section with No 0 and fill in with fairly bold runout icing. The holly and mistletoe are flooded with pale green icing. When colour is dry paint in the flower section with a

No 1 sable brush, shading the holly and mistletoe. Pipe holly berries with No 1 in Christmas red; when dry add a painted black spot in centre. Pipe mistletoe with No 1 tube in white. When dry brush lightly with snowflake petal dust.

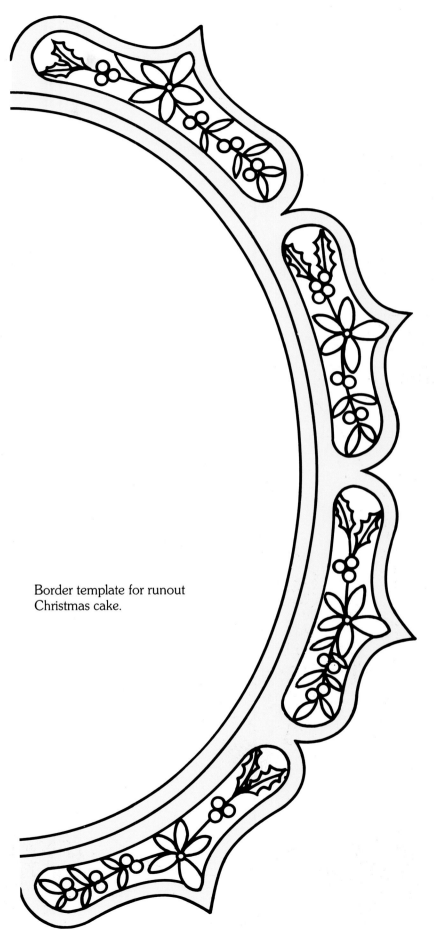

Border template for runout Christmas cake.

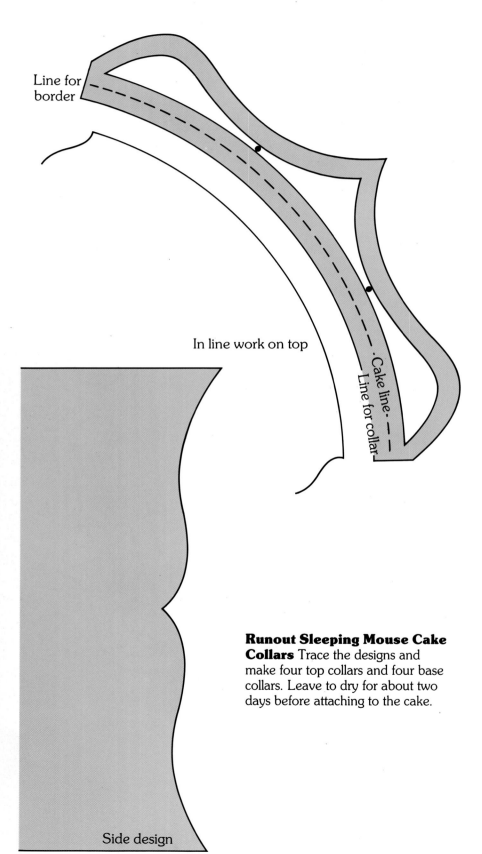

Line for
border

In line work on top

Cake line

Line for collar

Side design

Runout Sleeping Mouse Cake Collars Trace the designs and make four top collars and four base collars. Leave to dry for about two days before attaching to the cake.

The top design for the Sleeping Mouse Cake, which is piped directly onto the surface of the royal-iced cake. Transfer the design to the cake, then begin by piping the leaves which will appear furthest away when the design is finished. Build up the design with pressure piping (see page 40). Add in detail with a fine tube when the icing is dry.

Sleeping Mouse Cake

This enchanting cake would be suitable for either a birthday or a christening.

Coat a 20cm (8in) round cake with pale green royal icing, and coat the board with the same icing. Make the top and base collars and top design following the instructions opposite. Pipe the designs on the side. Position the base collars and neaten the edges with a snailstrail. Attach the top collars with royal icing and pipe dots on the inner edge. Place flowers between each collar.

Runout Greenhouse

Trace the pattern pieces and place under wax paper. Outline all the pieces with a No1 tube and green royal icing, then flood with soft royal icing. Let dry. Lie the front down and attach door. Pipe a line of royal icing for hinge. Position the door and support with foam rubber until dry.

Attach front to sides and sides to back, making sure the base lines match the plan with angles of 90°. When dry, attach the roof, side pieces and, finally, the top piece.

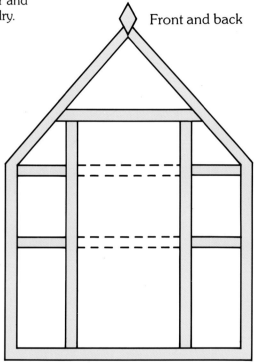

Front and back

Roof top

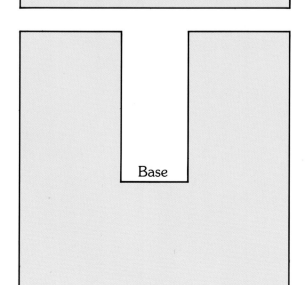

Base

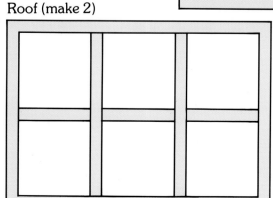

Roof (make 2)

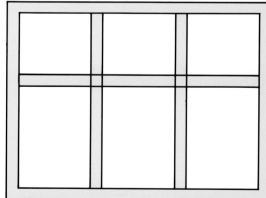

Side (make 2)

Door

Greenhouse Cake

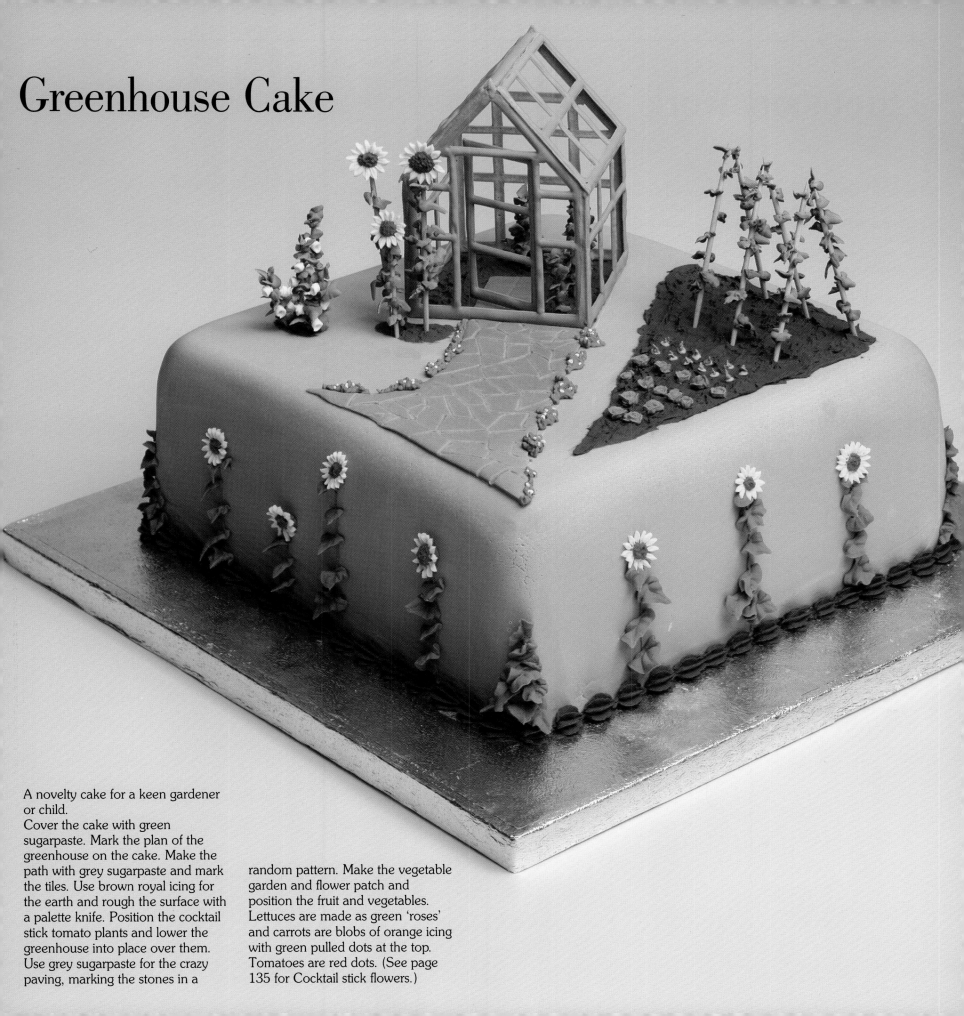

A novelty cake for a keen gardener or child.
Cover the cake with green sugarpaste. Mark the plan of the greenhouse on the cake. Make the path with grey sugarpaste and mark the tiles. Use brown royal icing for the earth and rough the surface with a palette knife. Position the cocktail stick tomato plants and lower the greenhouse into place over them. Use grey sugarpaste for the crazy paving, marking the stones in a random pattern. Make the vegetable garden and flower patch and position the fruit and vegetables. Lettuces are made as green 'roses' and carrots are blobs of orange icing with green pulled dots at the top. Tomatoes are red dots. (See page 135 for Cocktail stick flowers.)

Extension Work

Use fresh royal icing and No 00 or 0 tube for extension work.

Always work with the cake at eye level in a good light. Support your back with a small cushion to help prevent backache.

The first step is to pipe the bridgework, a ridge or bridge of icing piped around the edge of the cake from which the drop lines fall. The bridge is a series of drop loops, each row exactly over the preceding one.

To make a pattern for the bridge, measure a band of greaseproof paper the circumference of the cake, fold into sections and cut to the shape of the extension work. This can be scalloped just at the bottom or at the top and bottom. Put this pattern around the cake and mark the lines with a scriber. The bottom edge should be about 5mm (¼in) above the board. Pipe a snailstrail around the base of the cake with a No 0.

Work the bridgework with the cake tilted slightly away from you. Touch the tube to the cake at the highest point of the bridge, pull the tube away from the cake and,

maintaining even pressure, move the tube horizontally to the next highest point on the design. Touch tube to the cake again.

Work around the cake. Make sure the first row of bridgework is dry before starting on the second. There should be no gaps between the scallops and the cake. If there are, fill them by painting in soft royal icing with a fine paintbrush. Care must be taken not to pipe each row higher than the one before or an ugly cupped effect will result. Pipe each row exactly over the one preceding, just less than the width of a line.

When the bridge is completely dry, pipe the extension work. Tilt the cake towards you so that the lines fall perpendicularly. Touch the tube to the cake at the top of the design, then pull away immediately, taking care not to get a bulb at the top. Pipe vertical lines just beyond the bridge. Remove the ends with a fine, damp brush. The lines should be parallel and there should not be enough room to pipe another line between the strands.

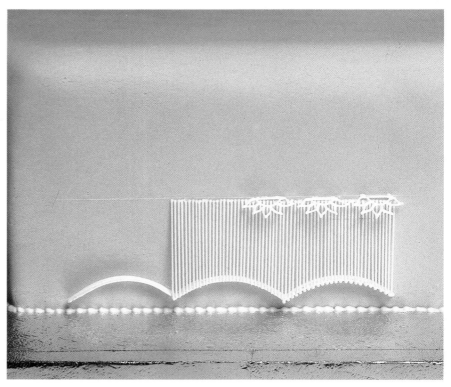

The simplest form of extension work is done with a straight top and scalloped lower bridge.

Another simple method is from a top line with points, and scallops at the bottom. Try piping dots onto the extension work. This is called hail spotting. Finish off with a triangle of dots, three at the top, then two, then one at the bottom. Pipe a snailstrail at the lower edge.

The bridge can be tapered at the sides. Pipe the first line of the bridge over the entire base line, each succeeding line should be piped slightly shorter. Pipe the last line to cover all the other lines. Great care must be taken to make sure each line is shorter by the same amount all around the cake.

For double extension with curtain effect, pipe basic extension work with hail spotting. Then pipe another five lines of bridgework over the first bridge. Tilt the cake towards you and slightly to one side. Pipe a second layer of lines. Finish off the lower edge with drop loops and pulled dots.

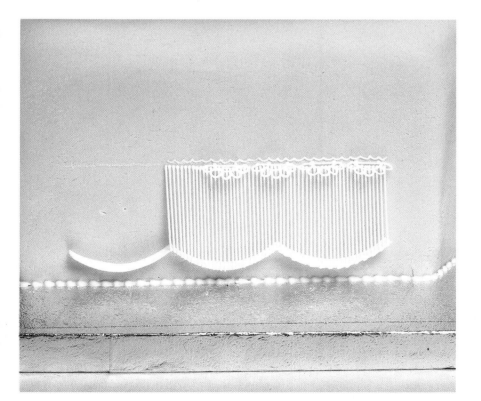

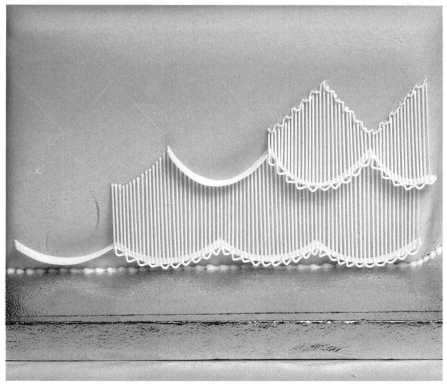

Pipe the bridge when the cake is upsidedown. Attach lace along the top edge and dots along the bottom.

For double extension work, pipe the first bridge and drop lines. Then pipe a second bridge as close as possible to the top of the extension work. Add a second row of extension work. The top and bottom edges are finished with drop loops.

Two-tier Cream Wedding Cake

Extension work without a bridge is done by piping from a line on the cake to the rim of a cake tin. When the icing is dry, the cake is removed from on top of the tin and the extension work remains unsupported. For a 20cm (8in) round cake, prepare a 23cm (9in) round cake tin by greasing the rim with white fat and place on the turntable. Put a 15cm (6in) upsidedown tin or dummy in the tin, and position the sugarpasted cake centred on it. The bottom of the cake should be about 5mm (¼in) lower than the rim of the tin. Pipe the extension work, taking great care not to knock the tin. Pipe dots to link each alternate line at the lower edge. Pipe more dots 1cm (½in) up the lines to link and strengthen them. Leave to dry. To remove, place a hand at each side of the cake and lift it straight up. Gently lower onto a prepared board.

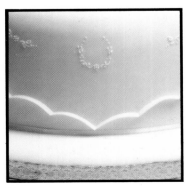

To create the unusual effect of points on the extension work the bridge must be piped with the cake upsidedown. Allow the sugarpaste to dry for at least 48 hours before attempting this or the surface of the cake will be damaged.

Cover two oval cakes in cream sugarpaste. Place a sheet of foam or several layers of smooth, soft cloth on a turntable. Carefully pick up the cake with the fingers of both hands spread out and pointing down. Turn the cake over and lower it onto the pad. Pipe the bridge in yellow and let dry. Carefully pick the cake up again, turn it the right way up, and lower it onto a prepared board. The extension work is piped in white with the cake the right way up using a No00 tube.

Position ribbons and side designs. Finish off with lace. Make the sugar flower sprays in complementary colours.

Tulle Extension Work

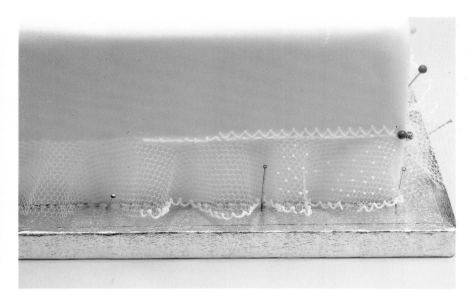

Cut a piece of tulle to the required depth and twice as long as the perimeter or diameter of the cake. Gather so that it fits snugly around the cake. Pin to the surface of the cake, then attach with a snailstrail. Pipe a scallop design at the top and bottom of the tulle, and finish by piping tiny dots on the tulle.

Mark the design onto the side of the cake. Cut tulle triangles slightly larger than the triangle in the design and pin to the cake. Attach with a snailstrail. Remove the pins when dry and finish off each piece with a snailstrail border. Pipe cornelli work on each triangle.

Cut and pin the tulle as above; attaching with a snailstrail. Finish off the bottom edge with a snailstrail and the top with scallops. Pipe cornelli work (see page 111) over the tulle.

Pipe the side designs and attach the ribbons first. Cut a piece of tulle to the required depth and twice as long as the perimeter or diameter of the cake. Gather so that it fits snugly around the cake. Pin to the surface, then attach with a snailstrail. Finish off the top with scallops, and pipe two rows of scallops around the bottom. Pipe tiny hearts on the tulle and attach heart lace above it.

Tulle Work Poppies

Tulle work involves cutting out shaped pieces of tulle, then piping the design with soft peak royal icing. Leave the pieces to dry over a curved surface if necessary, then attach to a plaque or cake with royal icing. Support until dry.

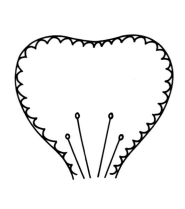

Cut four petals out of red tulle. Pin onto a greased apple tray or press foil into pastry tins and use foil cups. The petals should be pinned so that the outer edge bends back.

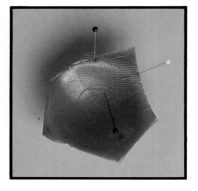

With red royal icing, pipe the design onto the petal and let dry.

Leaves: Cut out leaf shapes. Pipe the design and leave to dry flat or over a slightly curved surface. Pipe the stem directly onto the cake and when leaves are dry arrange them along the stem.

Pipe a blob of green royal icing about 5mm (¼in) in diameter onto the cake. Position the first two petals opposite each other. Support with foam or cotton wool. Place the third and fourth petals inside and on top of the first two. Push the petals into the green blob. Support until dry. Push black stamens into the centre blob as shown.

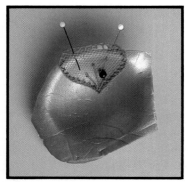

Tulle Work Key

Cut out the key in white tulle and place on a cake board. Cover with wax paper, then pin in position. Pipe the design. When dry, carefully remove from the wax paper, turn over and pipe on the reverse side. Let dry. Attach the key to the top of the 21st cake (overleaf) and support carefully with foam or cotton balls until dry.

Tulle Work Cradle

Cut out tulle according to a pattern. Trace around petal cutters to create your design and pin to a cake board over wax paper. Pipe the design and let dry.

Pipe the tulle base quickly onto wax paper and place over a curved surface, such as a kitchen roll tube. Tape each end to the roll.

When dry, attach one end to the base. Lay the outside of the end down on a flat surface. Pipe a line of royal icing in position. Attach base. Make sure it is level or the cradle will tilt. When dry repeat for the other end.

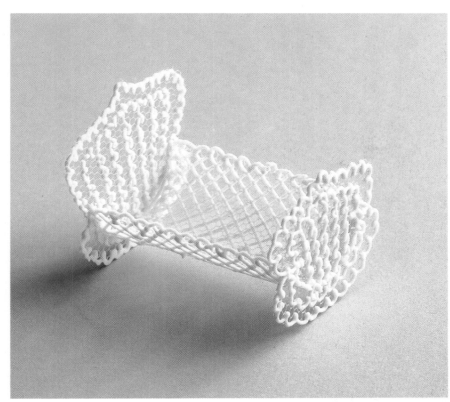

Twenty-first Birthday Cake

A delicately beautiful cake for a young woman.
Cover the cake in pale green sugarpaste. Place an oval of pink sugarpaste on top, outline with a pattern of three dots piped in a triangle; two at the bottom and one on top. Pipe lace: long, medium and short. Pipe embroidery onto the cake. Attach ribbon at the bottom and at a distance up the cake equal to the depth of the long lace. Attach the lace, supporting it with foam or cotton balls if necessary. Attach the key to the top with royal icing (see page 61). Support until dry. An easier way to do the key is to pipe it flat, directly onto the cake.

Lace

The addition of lace to a cake immediately gives it a delicate look. Lace is the last decoration to go on a cake, as it is very fragile. Always use fresh, well beaten royal icing or the lace will not be strong and will break as soon as it is picked up.

Lace patterns

Place the lace pattern onto a flat surface and masking tape a piece of wax paper over it. A very thin smear of white fat on the wax paper helps to release the dried lace. If the lace has a straight line where it joins the cake, pipe this first, then the rest of the pattern. When dry, the lace should come away easily. A slight movement of the paper should be enough to release the pieces, or use a thin palette knife or a fine brush. Pick up lace with your fingers (it is impossible to do this with tweezers) and attach to the cake with two dots of royal icing per section. This icing should also be fresh, well beaten to full peak or the pieces will not stay in place.

Lace Designs

The photographs and templates on the following pages show a variety of different designs for lace. When choosing a lace design, consider how it will fit in with the overall design of the cake. Although certain designs, such as hearts and bells, are traditional for a wedding cake, try snowflake lace for a winter wedding, or use lace which reflects the couple's interests, such as musical or sporting designs.

Remember that lace which looks simple may not always be the easiest to do. If it has just a few straight lines any flaws will show, whereas a more complicated design could mask faults.

Always pipe more lace than the design of the cake calls for to allow for breakages. If the cake is to be delivered, always take some extra lace on waxed paper and a filled piping bag wrapped in plastic as lace often gets damaged or drops off.

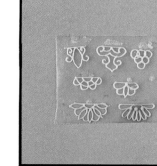

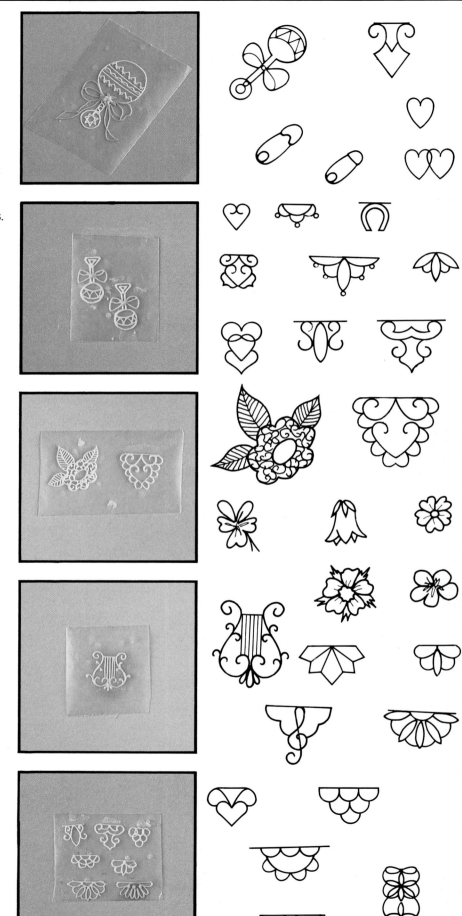

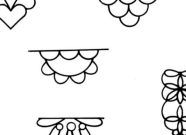

Two-tone Lace

To achieve these beautiful two- and three-tone lace pieces takes a little more time as two or three piping bags of the different coloured icing are used. However, the results are well worth the effort.

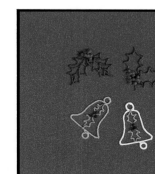

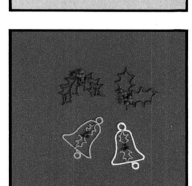

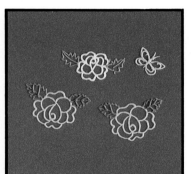

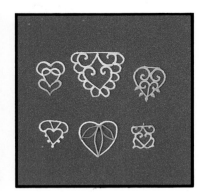

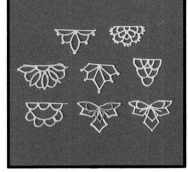

Cross-stitch Cake

Delicate, flowered filigree wings top this pale peach-coloured round cake. The top design is a filigree cross-stitch plaque.

Cover a round cake with peach royal icing. Stick cross-stitch plaque (see page 69) to centre of cake. Pipe trellis work and position wings (see page 69). Pipe a shell around the base of the cake with a No 43 tube and a rope following the shell with a No 2.

Trellis Side Designs

To pipe horizontal lines, tilt the cake towards you. A tilting turntable is ideal; alternatively put something like a roll of tape under the edge of the cake board to slightly raise the edge you are working on. Hold tube close to cake so lines do not droop.

Pipe angled lines starting with the left-to-right lines. Keep the angle the same throughout.

Cut a circle of greaseproof paper the same size as the cake; fold in quarters. Place on cake and mark where the folds meet the edge. Pipe a line from the top down the side to stick wings onto.

Pipe opposite angled lines on all sections.

Pipe four dropped lines onto the top and side of the cake as shown using a No 1 piping tube. Repeat on remaining three sections.

Pipe a small shell around top and base of each scallop with No 2 tube. Pipe a line following each scallop, and two dots at each point.

Pipe the vertical lines of the trellis on scallops in all sections.

Finish the cake by piping a shell border around the base. Outline with dot edging. A ribbon can be placed around the board if wished.

Lace Wings

Fragile sugar-lace wings give a dramatic finish to a cake. They are a bit tricky to handle and transport because they protrude from the cake. When designing lace wings, a balanced shape and main structural support are necessary, otherwise the wing could collapse when placed on the cake.

Pipe the other side piece.

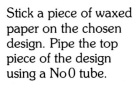

Stick a piece of waxed paper on the chosen design. Pipe the top piece of the design using a No 0 tube.

Continue piping until the top side is finished.

The finished wing with its three main pieces. Once dry, carefully remove from the waxed paper using a crank handle palette knife. Turn over onto a piece of foam which will act as a support and stop the wing moving about. Pipe the design on the other side to strengthen. Let wing dry before using, or store flat on thin foam.

Cross-stitch Plaque

This design was taken from a cross-stitch embroidery pattern. Once all the trellis work is finished, pipe small dots to match the pattern, using the colours shown. (See Cross-stitch Cake on page 66.)

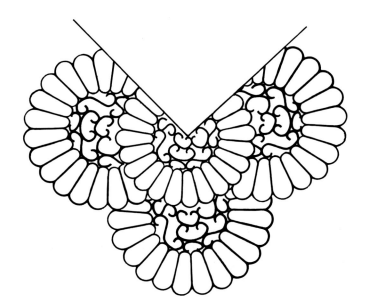

A double piped filigree wing as featured on the peach cake with cross-stitch plaque (see page 66).

Freestanding Birds

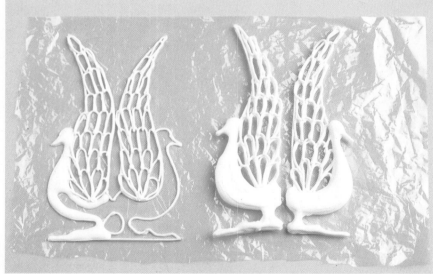

Outline the birds and wings with a No 1 tube; pipe in the wings with No 0 tube. Flood the head and body. Pipe two separate birds using the same pattern. When dry turn over and overpipe the loops of the wings with a No 0 tube. Flood the head and body. Leave to dry.

Lace Butterflies

Outline with No 0 tube, then fill in with firm light royal icing, piping lacy lines, rounds, etc. Leave to dry overnight.

Pipe the body on the cake and gently place the wings on the body. Sponge can be placed at each side until wings are firm.

Prepare a 10cm (4in) round thin board with floodwork. Stand the join section on the board with icing when it is completely dry. If it does not stand firmly place some sponge at each side. Join the two birds, one at each side. Decorate with thin ribbons.

Three-tier Rose Wedding Cake

A classic pink and white round three-tier wedding cake with an exquisite freestanding top ornament. This cake may be made without lace if wished. Make the top decoration as described opposite. Coat top and sides of cake with white icing, leave to dry. Cut template for sides, divide into eight sections. Pipe onto the cake and coat around bottom section with pink icing. Dry. Pipe frill with a No 59 tube. Two lines of lace are piped on the frill when dry. Pipe a top border of small shells with No 43. Overpipe loops with No 1. The bottom border is a shell piped upwards with No 46 and downward with No 43. Pipe loops as shown. The lily of the valley is piped straight onto the cake. Pipe roses and green leaves. Lace butterflies are added to centres as shown. (See also pages 132-134.)

Lace Inserts

Runout work can be given a softer look with lacy inserts. Design is important here to ensure the delicate work is not supporting the runout. Pipe the outlines, then the filigree or lace work, then flood in the runout area.

Designs for the lace inserts can be copied from fabric lace for a realistic look. Small lace pieces can be used to make pretty additions to large runout letters. Runout and lace work can be used as borders, collars, wings or flat top decorations for cakes. Handle the finished pieces carefully.

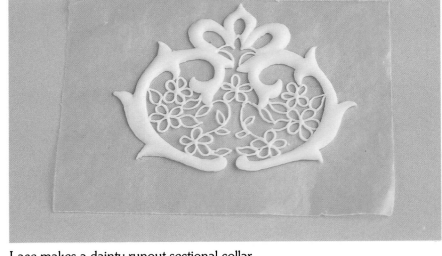

Lace makes a dainty runout sectional collar.

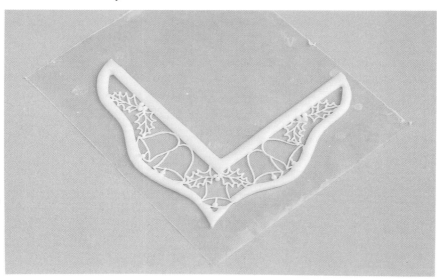

This corner section for a Christmas cake has a runout edge with lace work inside. It could also be done in colour.

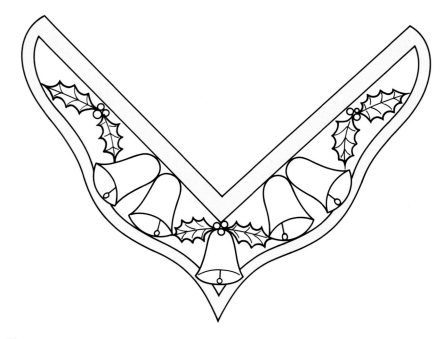

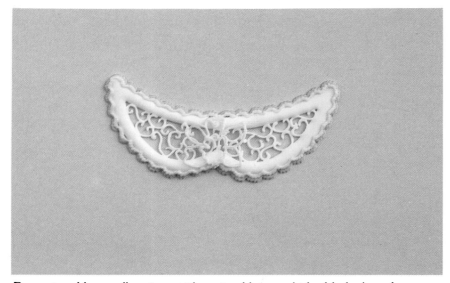

Runout and lace collar piece with a piped lace orchid added when dry.

Lace and Filigree Collars

Lace and filigree work can be used to make delicate collars. The fine piping is particularly attractive when combined with runout work, which gives the finished pieces more strength. These collars are very fragile, and choice of design is important so that the delicate work is not supporting the weight of the much heavier runout. It is a good idea to make at least one extra collar piece in case of breakages, especially if the cake must be transported.

To pipe a runout and filigree collar, pipe the runout outlines first, then do the fine lace or filigree work. Dry, then flood the runout areas. Dry the collar thoroughly before attaching to the cake.

For a filigree collar, place cellophane or waxed paper over the chosen design and pipe with No 0 or No 1 tube. Dry, then turn over and pipe on the other side for greater strength. It is best to keep these collars quite small and have several pieces to go around the cake.

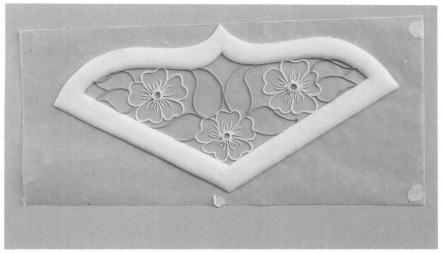

This runout collar features an inset of finely piped filigree flowers. Any flower design could be used.

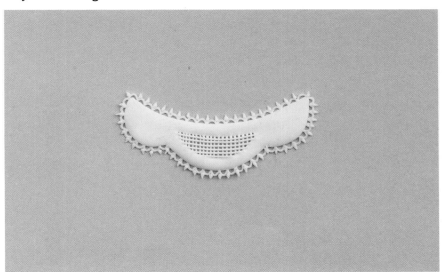

This sectional collar piece has trellis work piped with a No 0 tube into the inset. More elaborate designs could also be used.

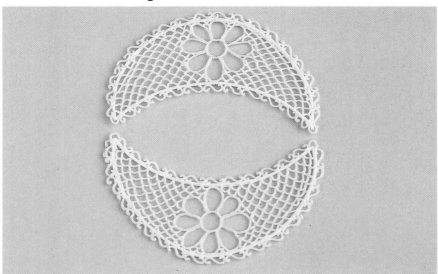

This pretty filigree collar makes a round cake into a petal. If used top and bottom, the gap between could contain piping.

73

Filigree

Filigree is ornamental work made of fine lines formed into delicate tracery. Light, showy and fragile, it makes a cake look very special. Place a suitable design or picture on a prepared runout board under fine cellophane or roasting wrap. Pin down, making sure the pattern is completely flat. Pipe with a No 00, 0 or 1 tube, or, for heavier work, a No 2.

Each piped line must touch another line or curve at some point or the tracery will break when you take it off the cellophane.

Leave to dry in a warm, dry, airy place for 48 hours before attempting to remove it from the cellophane. Do this with a very fine palette knife, pressed down towards the board.

Template for side panel

Pipe the birds first. Outline, then fill in with trellis and loops. Pipe the butterfly in lace. Pressure pipe branches to fill the whole area.

Use the pattern as a guide. Pipe flowers, buds and leaves with No 1 or No 0 tube, flower centres are piped with No 00.

Filigree Panel Cake

Pipe the rest of the lines the same way so that lines are now piped around the cake. Pipe lines with a No 1 tube down the next border. Finish with No 0 tube if wished. Add the side panels.

Pipe a line on each side with a No 43 tube the same shape as the runout panel. When dry overpipe to give the effect of a stand-off finish. Carefully put each side in place.

Coat cake four times with icing coloured pale blue with a touch of pink; leave a sharp edge. Make two hexagonal runout borders using the templates. Outline the edge of the lace top and the sides with a No 1 tube, then flood. Leave to dry.

Hold a few seconds until dry. Pipe a heart shape shell with No 43 tube down the corners and add butterflies. Finish bottom board with lines piped with No 1 from side panels to board. Pipe lines around plaque.

Place the large runout border on first. Pipe a line with No 43 at the centre edge, let dry. Overpipe and dry. Then add the smaller hexagonal border. When dry place sponge on three sections of the hexagonal border and rest the lace top on them. Keep the sponge small (under 1cm [½in]) and it will be easy to remove.

Pipe lines on the sections without the sponge, from top to bottom with a No 1 tube. When dry remove the sponge one section at a time.

Template for filigree top design

Filigree Panel Cake

This exquisite hexagonal cake is decorated completely in delicate filigree. The top design is actually a floating collar supported by fine line work.

Floating Filigree Plaque

Trace the wren design and place on a board. Cover with wax paper and tape down. Pipe the background using a No 00 tube. First pipe a straight line which goes through the centre of the circle. Turn 90° and pipe a second line at right angles to the first. Turn 90° and pipe a third line which is parallel to the first and 2mm (⅛in) away to the right. Turn 90° and pipe to complete the outline. Continue in this way until the grid is complete. Leave to dry.

Pipe the wren onto the grid lines. When dry, carefully remove from the wax paper and place gently onto a prepared circle of 2cm (¾in) foam cubes on top of the cake. The cubes should be about 1cm (½in) apart. Pipe lines from the edge of the plaque to the cake, carefully removing the cubes as you go. Pipe drop loops from the edge of the plaque, and position narrow lace around the bottom.

Filigree Plaque Cake

A delicately decorated cake, ideal for a special birthday celebration. Cover a round cake with pale lilac sugarpaste. Place on an iced cake card and position on a velvet-covered board. Pipe the side designs. Do the extension work without a bridge (see page 58). Pipe the floating filigree wren plaque and position. Add lace.

Crown Cake

A pretty mauve cake is topped with a filigree crown. Leave the crown plain, or fill with sugar or silk flowers.

Cover a cake with pale mauve royal icing. Make and position the crown. Pipe a small shell around the base of the crown with a No 1 tube. Use a No 0 tube to pipe forget-me-nots freehand over the top of the cake. Pipe a shell with a No 2 tube around the base of the cake. Place a contrasting ribbon around the side and attach sugar lace around the top edge. The gap between pieces should be about one-quarter of the width of the piece. Fill the crown with sugar flowers and ribbons.

Filigree Crown

The crown can be filled with a spray of pale pink carnations, mauve freesias and blossom.

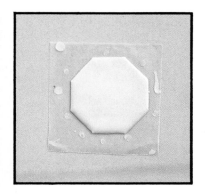

Outline base with a No 1 tube and flood.

When the crown is in position, complete the top designs on the cake. Place a ribbon around the middle.

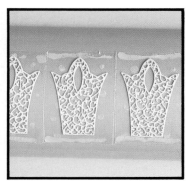

To make the eight filigree pieces, pipe outline with No 1 tube. Place over plastic pipe, then pipe a freehand S & C scroll filigree design into the space. Dry all pieces.

Pipe pale mauve lace with the same icing used to coat the cake. Attach as shown and leave to dry.

Stick the octagonal base onto the cake or plaque. Pipe a line along one side of the octagonal and place on a filigree piece. Use a piece of foam to support. Repeat with the next piece. Pull both pieces down so the two points touch and support at this angle. Pipe a small shell on the inside edge to strengthen and give a neat edge.

Continue with the other six pieces to complete the crown. Support each piece with foam. Leave for two hours.

Filigree crown - make 8

make 1

Runout octagonal base for filigree crown

Winged Crown

This design works best on a hexagonal cake as each of the six wings points to a corner making it easy to position them. You will need six of each of the two lace designs. The bunch of flowers is dried flat and the top pieces dried over a curve.

Three left and three right wings are needed. Pipe the outline onto waxed paper with a No 1 tube, and the inside filigree with a No 0. Transfer to a flat surface to dry. Another method is to make three copies of each wing pattern. The piped design can then stay on top of the pattern until it dries. When dry, turn over on foam and re-pipe the outer line only. Let dry. Pipe a line about 5cm (2in) long and place a wing in position. Support both sides with foam. Place the opposite wing into position. Pipe a dot of icing on the spots marked with a cross on the template and bring to touch. Keep wings supported with foam and clean excess icing from cake before it dries. Dry for one hour. Stick remaining four wings in place. Dry for 30 minutes.

Winged Crown Cake

Elegant pointed wings top a small
hexagonal cake. For a different look,
the wings could be placed flat on
the cake.

Cover a hexagonal cake in cream
sugarpaste. Place curved lace on
edge of cake, sticking on a fine line
of icing. Pipe a shell around base
with No 2. Pipe a small dot at
corners and place flat lace in
position. Place the crown on
top of the cake.

Oriental Stringwork

Oriental stringwork produces spectacular effects, and is not as difficult to do as it looks. Designs can be adapted from lace, knitting or crochet patterns. Oriental stringwork can be done in a single colour or in many different colours. For best results, always plan out and lightly mark on the cake where the loops are to go.

This is a method used to pipe borders on cakes using a fine tube. The cake is turned upsidedown and loops are piped which will stand up above the surface of the cake. Because the cake is handled more than usual in this technique, it is best to use a firm textured cake rather than a sponge.

First turn the cake upsidedown on a firm support whose diameter is smaller than that of the cake top. Use a small cake tin or a polystyrene dummy one size smaller than the cake.

Be sure each series of loops is dry before turning the cake.

1. Turn the cake upsidedown and place on a support. Pipe loops from the top edge of the cake and from the shell border. Leave to dry.

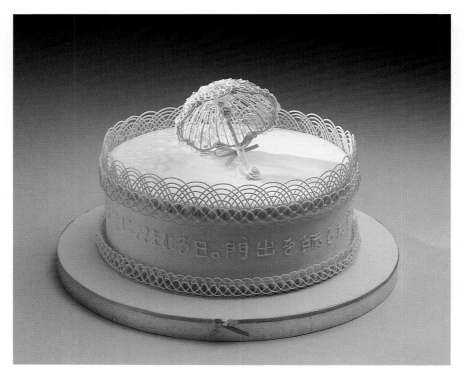

2. Pipe another series of loops overlapping the first around the top edge. When dry, turn the cake rightside-up.

3. Pipe dots as shown on the top edge.

5. Pipe loops between the dots around the top edge, and a similar row from the shell border.

4. Pipe loops to join the dots on the top edge. Pipe another row of loops from the shell border. The arch of the loops should just touch the board.

6. Turn cake rightside up and leave to dry before adding top and side decorations.

Lace Parasol

Any lacework pattern may be used for the parasol as long as all lines touch. Use any smooth ball of the correct size. Grease with white vegetable fat (shortening) to aid removal.

Pipe eight evenly spaced lines vertically from the top with a No 1 tube. Pipe scallops to join the eight sections.

Leave to dry overnight. Turn onto foam. It will come off easily when dry.

Pipe three lines in each section. Using a No 0 tube, loop round on top to form a flower. Pipe four rows of loops. Pipe lines down from the centre line to join sections at the base. Pipe scallops across and at base. Pipe scallops at base with a fine tube.

Place a small piece of flower paste in the centre. Pipe lines round. Attach painted cocktail stick with a flower paste handle. A bow and small rose may be added.

Oriental Stringwork Cake

The delicate lace parasol is a perfect complement for a cake decorated with fine oriental stringwork collar and border.

Coat the cake with a pale black-currant royal icing; finish with a sharp edge. Make parasol as described opposite. Pipe a shell border around the bottom of the cake as shown. Turn the cake carefully upside-down on a support. Pipe loops as described on pages 84-85. Place parasol on top leaning on its handle; stick with icing. Pipe oriental writing freehand on sides of cake in white.

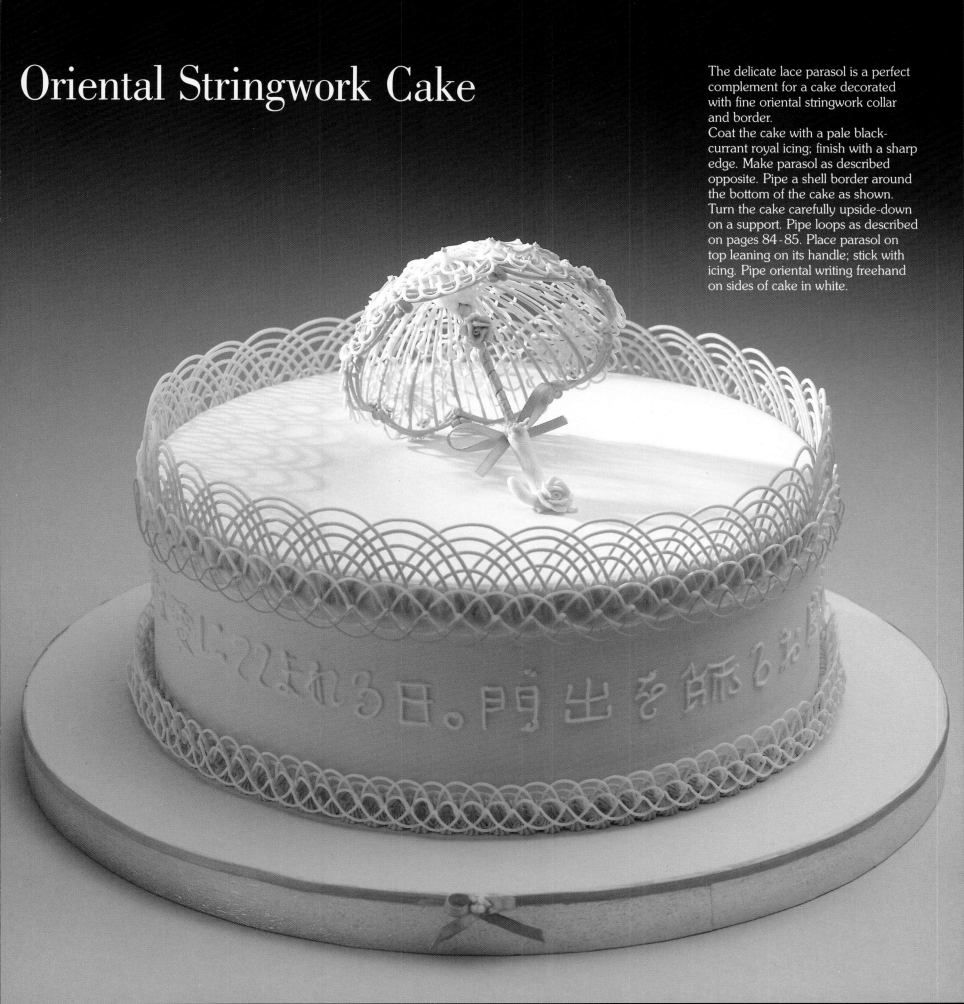

MODELLING

Using marzipan, sugar paste, pastillage and other pastes, modelling includes various techniques to produce all kinds of figures, pastillage greeting cards and outstanding bas relief work. These numerous ideas will also provide plenty of inspiration for your own individual models.

Apple cake: This charming novelty cake is made in the shape of an enormous apple. The mouse is life-sized.

Use a generous layer of marzipan when covering an awkward shape to eliminate all rough edges and bumps where the cake has been carved. Make any cavities larger than needed as each covering of sugarpaste will reduce its size. The marzipan can be built up or carved away at this stage to perfect the shape.

Fix the marzipanned cake to a board and cover completely with sugarpaste. Support paste with the hands as it is gently eased into the cavities. Cut away excess at base and smooth well with hands. Use a large soft brush to colour with red paste colour diluted with a little water and tinted with a bit of brown and green colour for a reddish-rust shade. Use large downward strokes; don't have the brush too wet. Copy a real apple for shading and detail.

Apply thinly rolled out cream coloured paste to the bite mark; indent with modelling tool to form marks. Paint marks a rust colour. Pinch out paste on edge to look like torn apple skin. Make stalk and leaves and add to top of apple. (See page 99 for mouse details.)

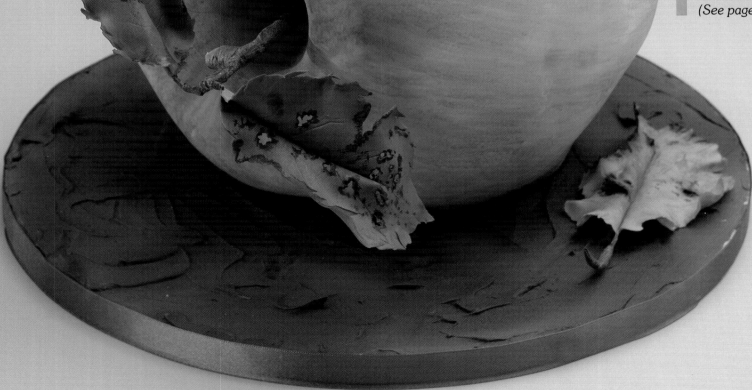

Recipes for Modelling Pastes

Mexican paste

Mexican paste is very adaptable. Figures can be moulded from it, or it can be mixed half and half with sugarpaste to make clothes for the figures. The same paste is used for bas relief.

225g (8oz/2 cups) icing (confectioner's) sugar, sifted
15ml (3 teaspoons) gum tragacanth
5ml (1 teaspoon) liquid glucose
30ml (6 teaspoons) cold water

Sift sugar and gum tragacanth onto a clean work surface. Make a well and add liquid glucose and cold water. Add 5 teaspoons of the water and only add the sixth if too firm. Taking sugar from the outside, start to mix the paste.

Knead until all ingredients are blended. If the paste is to be used for moulding bodies, add 15ml (3 teaspoons) cornflour (cornstarch) to paste and knead in. The paste made without the cornflour (cornstarch) will keep for about three weeks. The paste with cornflour (cornstarch) in it will only keep for 24 hours. If any is left over use it to make spare bodies, arms, etc to have in stock.

Pastillage

This strong paste is ideal for three-dimensional structures such as caskets.

10g (1/3oz) leaf gelatine
60ml (2fl oz/4 tablespoons) water
500g (1lb 2oz/4½ cups) icing (confectioner's) sugar, sifted
30g (1oz/¼ cup) cornflour (cornstarch)
30g (1oz) royal icing

Soak gelatine in water until softened. Warm over hot water until gelatine is dissolved. Make a well by sifting sugar and cornflour onto the work surface. Pour in water and gelatine solution. Mix. Add royal icing. Store in a polythene bag in a plastic container with a lid.

Gelatine paste

Gelatine paste is quick to make and very strong but it sets within 15 minutes of being made. Therefore all necessary equipment (templates, moulds, rolling pin, cornflour (cornstarch), knives, etc) must be assembled before making it, because of its short working life.

675g (1½lb/6 cups) icing (confectioner's) sugar
30ml (6 teaspoons) cold water
5ml (1 teaspoon) powdered gelatine

Sift sugar onto a clean work surface. Put water in a small, heavy saucepan (non-aluminium). Sprinkle with gelatine and dissolve over medium heat. Bring gently just to boiling point, remove from heat.

Use a wooden spoon to take about 15ml (3 teaspoons) sugar from the sieved pile and mix quickly with gelatine in the pan. Continue until mixture is thick.

Scrape mixture from pan to the middle of the pile of icing sugar. Knead quickly as it will start to set right away. Once the mixture resembles sugarpaste and is no longer sticky, place in a polythene bag. You may find it will not take all the sugar, so mix until it has taken up enough sugar to resemble sugarpaste consistency. Sift the remainder back into the pack when you have finished work. Wash your hands and move to a clean area of the work surface. Take a small piece of paste, roll out and cut or mould.

Modelling paste

This paste is used for making ornaments. It is not as strong as pastillage or gum pastes, but can be made quickly.

20ml (4 teaspoons) powdered gelatine
60ml (2fl oz/4 tablespoons) cold water
10ml (2 teaspoons) liquid glucose
450g (1lb/4 cups) icing (confectioner's) sugar, sifted

Sprinkle the gelatine on the water and leave to sponge. Dissolve over warm water until clear. Add glucose to clear gelatine and leave until melted. Make a well in the sugar and add the liquid. Stir with a small spatula or palette knife until well mixed. Knead until pliable.

Place in a polythene bag and leave for at least 3 hours before using. Ideally it should be left overnight.

Gum arabic glue

This glue is used for attaching clothes to bodies and for sticking soft pieces of paste to other pieces of soft or firm paste. It will dry more quickly than egg white. This glue does not keep well so make up a small quantity.

Mix 1 part gum arabic with 3 parts cold water. Leave to dissolve.

The same proportions, made with boiling water and left to cool slightly, will result in a glaze. Coat items 2-3 times for best effect.

Royal icing made without glycerine is used to join large structural pieces as it is stronger than egg white.

Instructions for Hedgehog Candy Box can be found on page 113.

Marzipan Characters

Each marzipan figure should have its own individual personality, with a different story to tell. By changing the facial expressions, particularly the eyes, and changing the colour and style of the hair, each figure becomes a unique character. If piping the eyes, always indent with a ball tool first. The noses are pink balls. The faces shown here can be adapted for both cutout and free-standing marzipan figures. See page 9 for homemade marzipan.

Pipe both eyes with pupils looking in the same direction. Position a small pink ball for the mouth, then place cocktail stick inside and rock it side to side. Shape yellow marzipan hair and mark with the back of a knife.

Pipe one eye and mark the other and the mouth with a half-moon tool. Shape red marzipan and mark the curls with the back of a knife.

A simple face marked with the halfmoon tool. Make sausages for plaits, snip ends and make tapered sausages for bows.

Pipe one eye and mark the closed eye with a half-moon marzipan tool. Use the same tool to mark the mouth. Cut black marzipan for the hair and place a tiny ball on top of the head for a bun.

Pipe eyes with pupils facing in the same direction. Position a small pink ball for the mouth, then place a cocktail stick inside and rock it up and down. Make a red tapered sausage and bend for the curls.

For a surprised expression pipe both eyes with the pupils looking up. Position a small pink ball for the mouth, then place cocktail stick inside and rock up and down. Make a red sausage and snip hair.

Pipe eyes with pupils facing inwards. Position balls for ears, indent with ball tool and marzipan strips for earrings. Coloured tapered sausages make the 'mohawk' haircut.

Baby

Make a 15g (½oz) cone for the body.

For the head, make a 5g (⅙oz) ball. Indent across the middle using the outside of your little finger, and mark the eyes with a ball tool. The ears are a tiny tapered sausage. Cut in half, taper into a question mark shape, attach and leave to set. The white baby's mouth is cut using a sharp knife. For the black baby, make a sausage, position on the face, insert a cocktail stick and rock gently from side to side. Pipe eyes.

For the legs, make a 3g (¹⁄₁₀oz) sausage. Indent with the outside of your little finger. Cut down the centre. Pinch up for the heel and mark toes. Position on body. The arms are a 2g (¹⁄₁₅oz) sausage. Taper one end, then roll with finger to make elbow and wrist. Cut down the centre, flatten the end for the hand, then cut for the fingers and thumb. Bend and position on the body.

Snooker Table

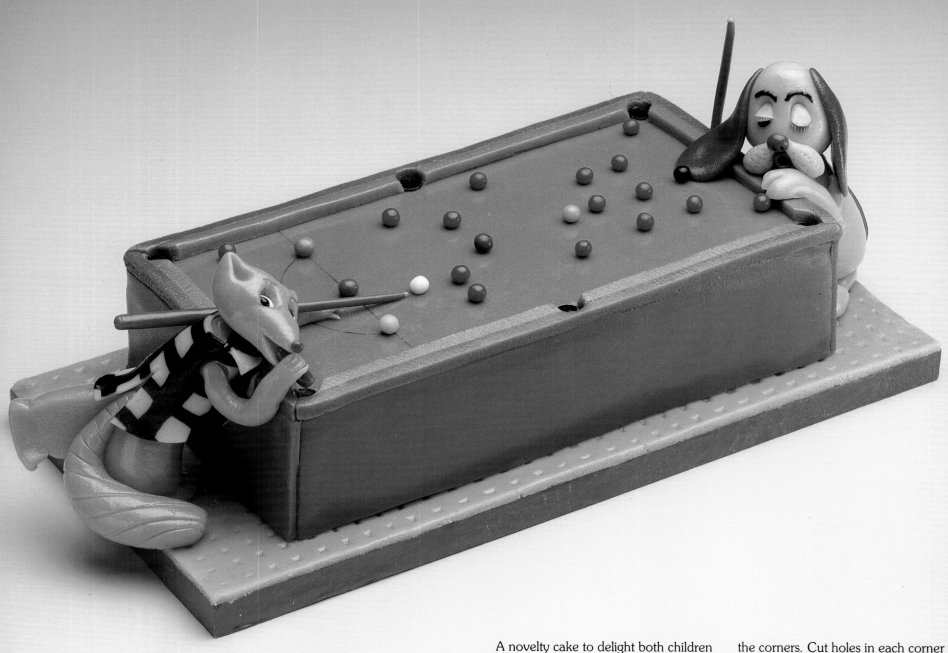

A novelty cake to delight both children and adults alike.

Cover a rectangular board with light brown marzipan and mark with a patterned roller. The cake is a 12.5cm × 25cm (5in × 10in) rectangle. Cover the sides with brown marzipan and the top with green marzipan. Make narrow strips of brown and green marzipan and put around the top edge, mitring the corners. Cut holes in each corner and in the centre of the long sides with a small round cutter, cutting halfway through the edges. Mark the holes with black marzipan. Make the coloured balls. Make the marzipan cues and leave to harden before positioning. Mark the lines on the table using a pen with edible ink. Position the figures of your choice.

Fox

Standing Mouse

For the body, make an elongated cone with 15g (½oz) orange marzipan. Cut pointed end of cone down the centre and bend legs over to shape. Mark paws with the back of a knife. Point the front end slightly for the neck.

Make a 5g (⅙oz) cone for the head and indent for eyes. The nose is a tiny pink ball. For the ears, make two tiny balls, position on the head, and indent with a ball tool. Alternatively, indent before placing on head, position pink balls for the inside, then position and indent again. Pipe eyes.

Tail is a 5g (⅙oz) sausage with a tapered end. Curve, then mark with the back of a knife. Attach to body.

Make a 15g (½oz) cone for the body. The feet are small flattened cones. Snip for toes, then place under body.

Make a 5g (⅙oz) cone for the head. Stroke up ears, then indent them and the eye sockets with a ball tool. Turn up the end of the nose and attach a small brown marzipan oval. Cut mouth. Use the end of a paintbrush to make a hole in the bottom of the head and place on neck end of body. Pipe eyes.

Make a 1g (⅓₀oz) sausage for each arm. Taper the top end, then flatten the other end for the hand. Snip for fingers and place around body.

Fisherman

The trousers and boots are made in one piece. Take a 20g (²⁄₃oz) yellow sausage and a 10g (¹⁄₃oz) black sausage and roll them together to make a long sausage. Cut three-quarters of the way down the middle to make the two legs and the seat. Bend to shape.

The fishing rod is a long, thin brown marzipan sausage. Leave to set very hard. Use sewing thread for the fishing line.

Make a 10g (¹⁄₃oz) pink ball for the head and make indentations for the eyes, nose and mouth. The nose is a pink ball. Make a small brown sausage for the moustache, taper the ends and position. Make a ball for the mouth, position, insert a cocktail stick and move gently up and down to open mouth. Ears are tiny pink balls. Position and indent. Add brown marzipan hair and mark with a knife. Pipe eyes.

Marble brown and white marzipan and mould into the log. Assemble the figure on the log and place on a thin cake board, or on top of a cake.

The sweater is a 15g (¹⁄₂oz) green cone. Make a green sausage and position for the poloneck. Make a 5g (¹⁄₆oz) sausage for the arms. Taper and cut in half. Make two small pink cones for hands. Flatten the ends and cut fingers.

The octopus is made from purple marzipan. Make a ball for the head and indent for the eyes. Press in a half-moon marzipan tool for the mouth. Pipe the eyes. Make eight long tapered sausages for the legs and arrange under the body.

Fish

For the body, make a 5g (⅙oz) yellow sausage and taper it slightly at one end. Make a small orange sausage, wrap it around the body and roll them together. Mark back with knife. Make an indentation with a cocktail stick at either side of the body and one at the end.

Make a green ball for the face. Flatten it and cut a triangle from the top. Place on body and indent for the eyes. Position a small yellow ball for the mouth, then place a cocktail stick inside and rock it up and down to make mouth open.

Make green flattened cones for the fins. Snip with scissors and place thin ends in indentations at sides. Make a larger cone for the tail, flatten, snip and position. Pipe eyes.

Crocodile

Take 20g (⅔oz) dark green marzipan, make a sausage for the head and body, and then elongate one end for the tail. Make the tail pointed by squeezing with finger and thumb. Cut with scissors to make scales. Use a ball tool to press along the sides of the body, then squeeze with fingers to make the ridges of the back.

Cut the mouth with a knife and press open. Make tiny white cones for the teeth and press into mouth with a cocktail stick. Make a red flattened cone and place in mouth for tongue. Make holes for nostrils with a cocktail stick and pipe. Make two small green balls for the eyes. Position, then make indentations with a ball tool. Place small white balls in sockets, then tiny brown balls for pupils.

Make two small sausages, indent for legs. Cut in half lengthwise, mark the feet and press out with fingers. Attach to sides of body.

Frog

For the body, make a cone with 20g (²⁄₃oz) green marzipan. Flatten top slightly for head.

For the legs, make a sausage with 5g (¹⁄₆oz). With the outside of the little finger, indent to show thigh and ankle. Cut lengthwise. Flatten one end of each leg to form feet and cut for toes. Attach legs to body and bend into position. Place a tiny ball of marzipan on each toe. Use 2g (¹⁄₁₅oz) marzipan for both arms and make as for legs.

A simple way of making the bride's veil is to cut a petal shape from thinly rolled sugarpaste or marzipan and then mark the lace pattern by pressing in with a decorative button or similar item. The groom's jacket can be made by cutting a circle from black marzipan. Cut a smaller circle for the neck, mark with a knife, and wrap the jacket around the figure.

For the head, make a cone with 5g (¹⁄₆oz). Flatten the end for the mouth and cut with a sharp, pointed knife. Place point of knife in mouth and press down to open it. Squeeze sides to make a smile, then use small end of ball tool to press in the sides. Use finger and thumb to press and stroke top of head to form eyebrows. Make indentations with a ball tool for eye sockets and pipe eyes. Make indentations for nostrils with a cocktail stick. For the tongue, make a cone from red marzipan, flatten it, mark a line down the centre with a cocktail stick, and position tongue in mouth.

Mouse Wedding Cake

A pretty cake for a small wedding. Cover an oval cake with white sugarpaste. Position a white frill (see page 21). Make the three mice (see page 93) and dress them following the instructions opposite.

Sugarpaste Modelling

Although moulds are available for making modelled figures, more individual and lifelike results are gained by making them freehand and with an armature (wire support). This ensures that no two figures are alike. Each one takes on a personality of its own as choices of pose, features, dress and size are made.

Because the figures do vary in size and shape, the clothes patterns need to be adapted individually. Make the paste garments larger than needed so that the paste can be trimmed to shape as it is being draped around the form.

As the figure is dressed, it will increase in size, therefore the paste should be kept as thin as possible. Also the body shape should start off narrow to allow for the bulk of added clothes.

Accurate figure proportions are important. The head should measure one-sixth of the body height. In the case of a child, however, the head size is a little larger. Arms with outstretched fingers reach to mid-thigh.

Asking someone to pose will help to achieve a natural position.

A model made with a wire armature should not be used as a decoration on a cake for children or elderly people as they may attempt to eat it.

See page 12 for sugarpaste recipe.

Painting the features

Eyes should focus on an object within the scene so they don't seem vacant or staring. Indent the socket and whiten. When dry paint the coloured iris. Dry, then place the pupil inside. A white dot can be added for a highlight. Carefully outline with a very fine brush, then add lashes and brows.

Blush cheeks with dusting powder. Paint lips a pale paprika colour; not bright pink or red.

Pipe hair with royal icing; or make by pushing soft paste through a garlic press or sieve. Alternatively, roll very thin sausages of paste into fine strands. This last method looks effective but is time consuming.

Each modelled part must be allowed to dry completely, otherwise it will crack and disintegrate when you try to dress it.

Snowman

Make a cone of white paste for the body and a ball for the head. Arms are two sausages, each indented at one end for mitts. Roll out a piece of coloured paste and cut a long, thin strip for scarf. Fringe each end and wrap around neck. Paint features. Indent a hole for the nose and insert a thin stick of orange paste for carrot. Indent a hole in mouth to hold pipe made of a tiny black sugarpaste sausage flattened at one end. Roll a large pea of black paste for hat. Shape into a cone.

With fingers pinch out bottom edge to form brim. Keep turning and pinching until hat takes shape. Indent top with a large ball tool. Pinch and furl brim. Make mitts of brightly coloured paste and place in arms. Make a long brown sausage for broom handle; leave to dry. For twigs, cut thin pieces of paste and stick together with royal icing or very sticky modelling paste. Hide join with a thin sausage of brown paste wrapped around the end of the twigs where they join the handle.

Cat

Make cone for body from sandy coloured paste. Cut a section up the front with a sharp knife, divide in

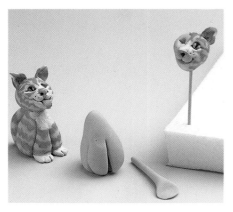

two for legs. Pull legs downwards, indent and pinch to form feet. Cut toes. Make a ball of paste for head. Indent eyes. Cut nose and mouth with scalpel. Open mouth with modelling tool. Add tongue. Cut a triangular piece of paste for ear. Pinch top corner, indent with ball tool, pinch the lower edge together and attach to head. Make a long sausage for tail; taper to a point at one end. Attach to body and drape over shoulder. When dry, paint stripes with paste food colour.

Mouse

To make the fat mouse on the Apple Cake, make a large, fat cone. Position a cocktail stick to hold the head, and make the head as for the other mouse.

Head is a small cone. Indent eyes, nostrils and a tiny mouth. For ears, press a ball of brown and a ball of flesh coloured paste together. Indent with ball tool. Pinch together base of ear and attach to head.

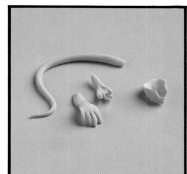

Make the paws, tail and ears as for the other mouse. Attach ears to head, but do not fix paws and tail until mouse is in place.

Texture the surface of the paste with a scalpel, or use royal icing piped onto the mouse and brushed to look like fur.

The apple leaves are finely rolled sugar-paste mixed with gum tragacanth. Frill the edges with a cocktail stick, and cut 'worm holes' with a piping tube. Attach to florist's wire.

For back legs, make a ball, flatten and pull out to form top of leg. For front paws make a small cone; indent with little finger and curve to form arm. Make hands and feet with a small sausage of dark flesh colour. Flatten and cut four long, thin fingers and toes. Place on foam and indent with a ball tool to curve fingers. Attach to arms and legs with gum arabic glue. Blend with modelling tool.

The shape of the apple is made by moulding the marzipan around the cake. The indentations for the stem end and the eaten portion should be carved out of the cake. These cavities should be quite large as with each covering of marzipan and sugarpaste they will reduce in size.

Make a long, thin sausage of dark flesh coloured paste for tail, tapering at one end. Using dark brown paste, make a thin pointed cone for body.

Paint lines on the eaten portion of the apple with food colouring. Position the mouse, then attach his paws and tail. See page 88 for finished Apple Cake.

Puss in Boots

As this is a large piece of modelling it will need a heavy plaque base. Make a wire armature for the body using 24-gauge wire. Mould paste around the wire. Exaggerate chest, keep waist narrow and slightly build up sides of thighs. Leave to dry.

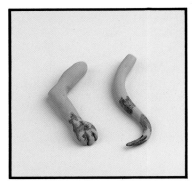

Model arms, paws and tail. Place in desired position, paint details of fur and leave to dry. Dress figure.

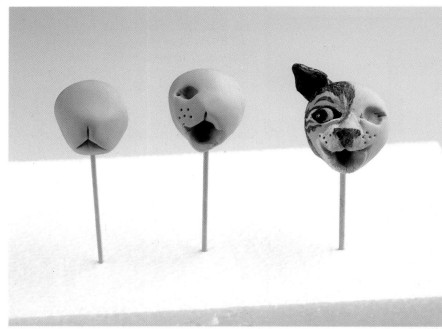

Mould face. Pinch nose, indent eyes and open up mouth. Model one ear and attach to head.

Leave to dry, then attach head to body with royal icing. Paint features.

For boots, make a fat sausage of brown paste, indent centre with finger and bend in half. Model one end to form foot by working on a flat surface. Pinch in toe and round heel. Place a modelling tool inside top of boot and start to open. Keep pinching and turning the boot until it is the desired height. If the top has frilled too much, make a pleat on the inside. To make cuff, cut a thin strip of paste and glue inside top of boot. Round off top edge. Make creases with a modelling tool to give a worn look. Attach arms to body. Paint details on clothing, stripes on trousers, etc. For sack, make a large ball of earthy or sandy brown paste. Start pinching top edge, open up slightly with a modelling tool. Make creases and bulges. Arrange to sag against Puss's boot.

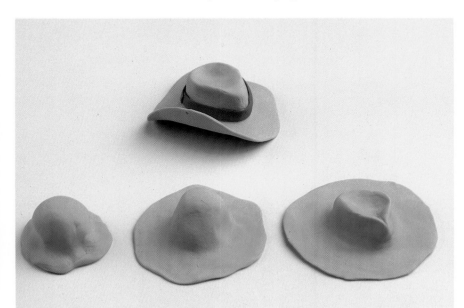

Make a ball of paste for hat. Roll into a thick sausage, pinch out top. Keep turning and pinching until the brim is the desired size and thickness. Open up crown with a ball tool. Indent top with finger and pinch together. Place on Puss's head and tilt front brim at a rakish angle. Add buttons, scarf, belt and buckle, hat band, tongue, etc. Sprinkle coloured gelatine crystals on plaque for path and muddy area. Add grass and moss of green paste.

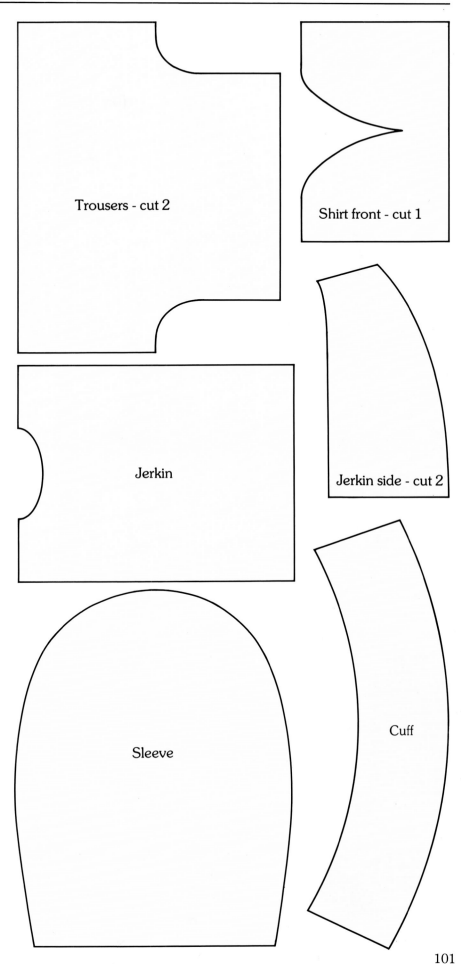

Trousers - cut 2

Shirt front - cut 1

Jerkin

Jerkin side - cut 2

Sleeve

Cuff

Father Christmas

Make a red cone for body. Make two red balls and flatten for legs. For boots make a black sausage, indent in middle with little finger and flatten bottom edge of sole to give shape. Assemble body, legs and boots. Make arms as for Snowman on page 98.

Attach small ball of flesh coloured paste for head. Make cone of red paste for hat. Pinch top to give shape. Paint features. Pipe in beard and fur edging. Add a small ball of red paste for nose.

For sack, make a large fat sausage of brown paste. Indent with finger. Rotate sack while pinching with fingers to open up. Pinch two corners at base and flatten sack so that it will stand. Model presents and toys to fill.

Make a large sausage in pale brick coloured paste for chimney. Flatten each side to form a square. With a scalpel remove a section of paste from inside chimney top. Leave chimney to dry. Paint in bricks with paste colour. Insert logs and boots or arm. Pipe snow with soft royal icing.

Christmas Tree

Elaborate Choirboy

Roll out red paste 2mm (⅛in) thick. Make a cone, leave to dry.

Roll out white paste thinly for surplice. Cut lower edge with No 2 and 3 writing tubes. Attach to cone.

Make a tall cone. Using a sharp, fine bladed pair of scissors, cut paste into points. Start at the base and work upwards. The points become smaller towards the top of the tree. Make sure there are no gaps between them.

To make arms, taper one end of a flesh coloured sausage and flatten to form a spade shape. Cut out thumb and fingers. Roll with index finger and thumb to form wrist, elbow and upper arm. Leave to dry. Wrap red paste around arm to form sleeve. Cut out surplice sleeve from white paste. Make patterned edge as for bottom of surplice. Drape sleeve around arm and attach to body with royal icing.

If the tree is made of green paste it can be decorated with coloured baubles of icing, parcels, and a star attached to the top point. Dredge with icing (confectioner's) sugar for a snowy effect. If the paste has not been coloured, dust with silver snowflake dusting powder.

Make ball for head. Pinch a nose. Indent eyes slightly. Make mouth by inserting cocktail stick into the paste. When dry, paint features. Dust cheeks a rosy colour. Pipe some hair with royal icing. Make frilled collar by cutting out two shapes with a small carnation cutter. Frill edges with cocktail stick. Place collar, then head on cone.

103

Cameo Plaques

Colour the sugarpaste by adding a touch of black to pink, green or blue. Roll out the coloured paste on a little icing sugar. Make sure all icing sugar is rubbed off the surface of the paste to leave an eggshell finish.

Cut out plaques in round or oval shapes. Press the pattern from an empty perfume bottle or similar to form an impression.

Cut around plaque again as when you make the impression you will lose the shape of the original plaque. Leave to dry.

Start piping from the top of the figure (head) and press, using a bag fitted with a No 2 tube and filled with normal royal icing.

Press the head round and downwards to form the neck. Pressure pipe the arms next and shape the body. Fill in.

Pipe the legs using a greater pressure for the section above the knees; the pressure is less for the lower leg and the feet.

The fine parts, such as hair, branches etc, are piped with a No 0 tube.

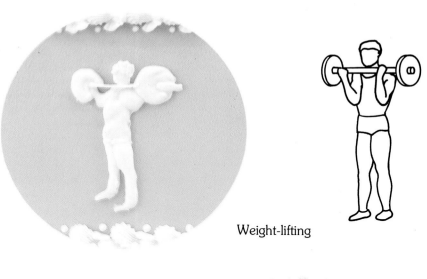

Weight-lifting

Discuss throwing

All impression cameo figures are done in the same way; bodies filled from head to toe with No 2 and the extras with a No 0 tube. Plaques with other subjects, such as love birds, can be done in the same way.

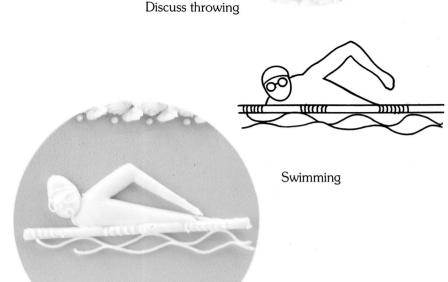

Swimming

Sport Cake

This unusual design features cameo-style runouts representing different sports. Other designs could be copied from photographs.

Coat the cake in green icing. Make runout figures for the sides. The fencers are piped, turned over when dry and flooded on the back. Place a small piece of cocktail stick up one leg leaving 15mm (½in) to push into the cake. The sword blades are wire.

When dry mask and wires are piped with No0. Place fencers in position. Pipe a heart shape shell border with a No43 tube and add dots and white leaves with No1. The five ring Olympic emblem is piped with a No2 tube. The torches are runout, both sides of the flame made of icing brushed into shape. These are added last.

Making Moulds

Years ago moulds were made of sulphur or plaster of Paris. Today new compounds are available which are not so messy or time consuming. The two main choices for mould making material are self hardening or oven drying. The latter is quicker as moulds can be made, baked and used as soon as they have cooled. The self hardening compound is not as useful since large pieces can take up to two weeks to dry. It is also slightly porous and easily damaged.

Moulds made of the oven drying compound are strong and will last forever. The compound can also be used for making decorating tools, such as formers for flowers and leaf veiners.

Knead the compound until it is pliable. Take a piece large enough for making the mould – it must be thick enough to take the depth of the figure and large enough across to take its width. Choose the figure carefully. It should have no cut away areas that would make it difficult to remove after being pressed into the compound.

Form compound into a block. Coat the figure with vegetable oil and press in firmly. Do not move the figure around or definition of the design will be lost. If the identation is not satisfactory, remould the compound before baking. Pull out the figure, place compound on a baking tray and put in the oven. Refer to manufacturer's instructions for baking time and temperature. Remove from oven and cool.

Rose and Leaf Mould

Knead a piece of baking clay until pliable and roll into a ball. Roll out slightly, making sure it is thick enough to contain the item to be moulded. Brush item with vegetable oil.

Push item into the clay, pressing straight down and trying not to wiggle the object as this will make a double impression. Push down until surface is level with the object. Bake in oven as explained opposite. Cool.

Finished rose. The green paste leaves were put in first by making teardrop shaped pieces of paste and squashing them into the leaf part of the mould. The peach paste was then pushed into the rest of the mould. The flower can also be made of white paste and painted when dry.

Swans

For wedding cakes, fill swans with ribbons and flowers; for christenings use swansdown and a paste baby or toys.

The equipment needed for making a swan. Use Mexican paste, see page 89.

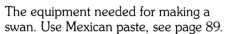

Cut the mould in half and dust with cornflour (cornstarch). Roll out a piece of coloured paste and drape into half of the mould.

Cut off excess paste. Take out swan and dust a little more cornflour (cornstarch) in the mould to ensure the swan does not stick. Make sure the edge of the paste is even and level with the top of the mould. Let dry in mould for about four hours.

Repeat the process on the second half.

Brush some egg white on the soft (second) half and place the two halves together, using paper clips to hold in place. Leave to dry overnight. Take off paper clips and carefully remove moulds.

The finished swan has been dusted with silver snowflake lustre powder to give a silky effect.

Decorating Moulds

These white paste figures show how food colours and petal dust can be used. Painting finished figures is quicker than colouring paste and also saves waste which occurs when too much paste is coloured.

Car. Painted red with black and then silver.

Children. Night-clothes are painted with pink and blue colour mixed with clear spirit. Cheeks are dusted with pink petal dust and hair is painted.

Horse. Painted dark brown with white and grey detail.

Horseshoes. One is painted with pink petal dust mixed with clear spirit. The other is painted with silver dust and clear spirit.

Tiny babies. These babies can be used for christening cakes and cradles. Make a mould using a small, plastic sleeping baby. Use mould to make babies of white paste. Paint one pink with blonde hair and the other blue with brown hair.

Goldfish. Painted with gold lustre colour and a small amount of orange colour mixed with clear spirit.

Tortoise. Painted brown and black.

Christmas tree. This was painted with green colour mixed with clear spirit. Tub is red and baubles and decorations are silver.

Buttons

Side designs.
These pieces are made with special moulds designed for this purpose. Several pieces will be needed to decorate a cake.

Buttons come in so many unusual designs and shapes that they are excellent for making small moulds. They can also be used for embossing the surface of a cake.

Rabbit. This rabbit was made using a mould. Let dry then colour by painting with brown colour mixed with clear spirit. Shade ears pink, and mix white petal dust with clear spirit and a little pink colouring to paint the nose. Stick two small balls of paste onto the face with egg white for eyes. Paint in pupils. Mix black food colouring with an equal amount of edible varnish and paint nose and pupils to make them shiny.

Knead the clay until soft and pliable. Roll into a ball. Choose a button. Brush with a little vegetable oil and push into the clay until it is level with the surface. Remove button. Bake the clay to harden the mould, then cool. Push coloured paste into mould and use a cocktail stick to lever it out. Trim off excess paste with a modelling knife if necessary.

Bells

Bells can be used on all kinds of cakes, from wedding to Christmas cakes. They can be filled or left plain. Half bells make an interesting decoration.

Use pastillage or gelatine paste (see page 89). Dust the inside of the mould with cornflour (cornstarch). Roll out paste to about 10mm (⅓in) thick.

Place paste into mould. Push into the centre of the mould. Continue pushing until paste has taken the shape of the inside of the bell. Keep taking paste in and out to be sure it is not sticking. If necessary dust the inside of the mould again with cornflour (cornstarch).

Use a small sharp knife to trim away excess paste. Use your index finger to smooth the edge of the paste to a fine edge.

Leave bell in the mould for about ten minutes before turning out to dry. Leave six hours before decorating.

Half Bells

These two bells are half relief, which makes them ideal for decorating the side of a cake. They also give an unusual look to the top of a cake. Careful moulding is important as cracks on the surface will make it difficult to paint the design.

Mould the bell following the instructions, but cut in half while still in the mould, using a modelling knife. Be careful not to damage the mould. Alternatively, remove bell from mould, cut and replace immediately. Leave in mould for about 15 minutes to harden. Remove and dry thoroughly. Paint or pipe a design onto the surface.

The larger bell has a painted holly design. Thread a piece of ribbon under the bell before sticking it down so it appears to be hanging. Pipe in a gong and some dropped lines. If bells are attached on top of a cake, carefully tilt the cake on the turntable so the top of the bell is higher than the bottom, then pipe the dropped lines.

The smaller bell is painted with a dainty floral pattern and finished off with a small bow.

110

Filled Bell

Cornelli work is useful for disguising a faulty iced surface, decorating a cake board or as part of a cake design.

Make some ribbon loops.

Stick a ball of rolled sugarpaste about the size of a walnut into the bottom of the bell. Fill with a circle of ribbon loops, alternating colours. Finish off with ribbon tails.

Use tweezers to add sugar or fabric flowers to fill the gaps.

The bell ready to stick onto the cake top. Prepare some lace, let dry completely. Use a No 0 tube to pipe a small line on the top outer edge of the bell; place one piece of lace in position. Work round and under the lower edge of the bell. To attach the lace to the base of the bell, pipe a line, then use a dry No 3 or 4 paint-brush as tweezers. Push lace into the bristles, touch onto the line of icing and pull away brush.

Use a small piping bag fitted with a No 0 tube to pipe cornelli work up to 2cm (¾in) on the inside of the bell. The rest will be filled with ribbon loops and flowers. Place the bell on foam to stop it from moving about. Let dry for about 30 minutes.

The finish bell, filled with ribbon loops and flowers and decorated with a row of sugar lace.

Place upturned bell on kitchen towel. Pipe cornelli work over the outside surface; let dry for two hours.

Cornelli work. This is a piped continuous wavy line, using a No 0 or No 00 writing tube. The line has no sharp angles and all the lines are equidistant from each other, producing a delicate pattern.

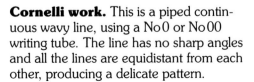

111

Hedgehog Box

Copy the pattern for the box. Roll out white pastillage or gelatine paste and cut out four hexagonal pieces and six side pieces. (Two extra side pieces are made in case a mistake occurs when painting the design.) Dry all pieces flat. Turn over after 12 hours to dry reverse side.

Assemble with royal icing onto waxed paper. Stick base and inner base together. Attach lid. Paint a freehand or scribed design on the side pieces. Place base on wax paper. Place side pieces into position, support with sugar lumps or piping tubes until dry. Pipe shells on inside edges for strength and support. Pipe a shell with a No 2 tube around the three edges and up the sides of the panels.

On a separate piece of wax paper, pipe round the edges of lid. When dry, place silk inside box and fill with chocolates, sweets (candy) or petit fours.

Colour box lid with green food colouring. Stick on hedgehogs. Add some moulded toadstools and grass. Transfer to a velvet covered board for presentation. (For the paste recipes, see page 89.)

Hedgehogs

To decorate the box shown, make one large and two small hedgehogs. Make a cone of brown Mexican paste and pull up slightly for snout. Cut a slit for the mouth and make indentations for eyes and ears with a ball tool. Mould ears and stick in position with egg white. Mould four feet, cutting each at one end for toes. Stick in position. Mould nose and attach. Roll two small balls of white paste for eyes; place in sockets.

Each spine is rolled between the fingers. Start at the base and stick on all the way round; work outwards slowly. It will take a day to make this top so allow plenty of time. Let dry.

Dust a mixture of brown and black petal dust. Paint face with food colouring as shown. Mix black food colouring with an equal amount of edible varnish and paint nose and pupils to make them shiny.

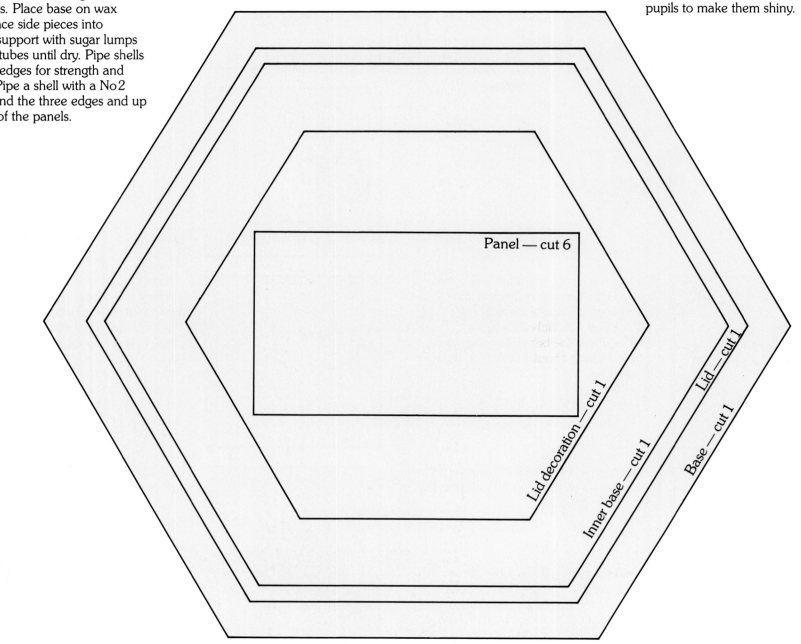

Panel — cut 6

Lid decoration — cut 1

Inner base — cut 1

Lid — cut 1

Base — cut 1

Hedgehog Candy Box

A wonderfully impressive gift, this box is made from cut-out pastillage pieces and assembled, then topped with modelled hedgehogs. If stored carefully, wrapped in tissue paper and left in a cool place, the box should last a long time.

Pastillage Greetings Cards

Pastillage can be used to make wonderful, original greetings cards for any occasion. The card can be placed on a cake, or it can be boxed and presented as a gift.

A simple pastillage card can be just a flat cutout rectangle or square with a piped or painted message. More interesting designs use cutout shapes, bas relief figures, or, like the card shown here, are in two parts and can stand up. Copy a real card, or draw your own designs.

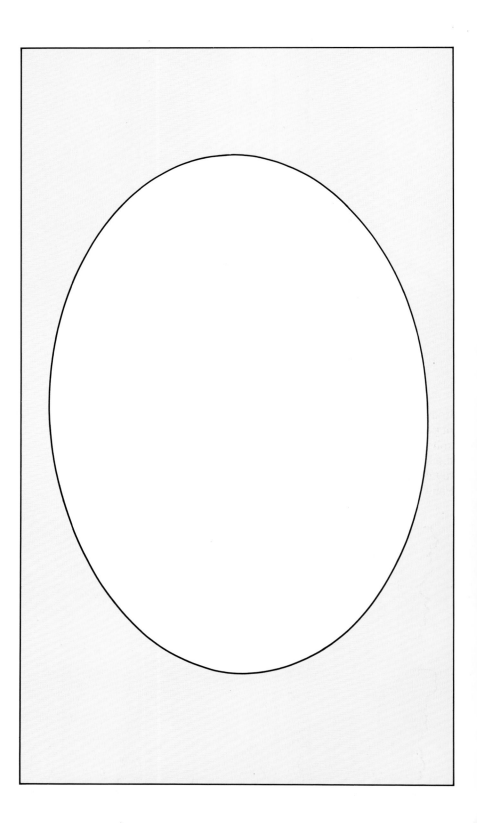

Card – cut 1 solid and one with cutout window.

Roll out flower paste (*see* page 140) or pastillage paste and use a sharp knife to cut out the pieces following the templates. Leave to dry, turning regularly to ensure they dry evenly. Paint the design on the bottom half.

Using royal icing and a No 1 tube, pipe cornelli work (*see* page 111) on the top piece. Pipe a lace edging round the outside edge and the cutout oval.

To assemble the card, pipe a fine line of royal icing along the edge and position the top piece onto the bottom piece at an angle. Support with foam until completely dry. Attach pastillage butterflies, and place another butterfly on the front of the card. Stand up when dry.

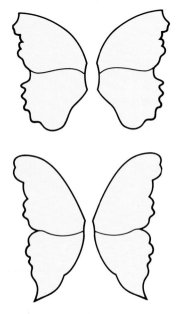

Butterfly wings templates

Fuchsia Card

This modern piece is made of pastillage and flower paste (see page 140).

Roll out pale green pastillage to about 3mm (⅛in) thick. Cut out following the template. Roll out grey paste and cut out using the template. Dry both pieces flat for 24 hours, turning after 12 hours.

Trace fuchsia design onto greaseproof paper, scribe onto the grey plaque. Roll out some flower paste very finely and cut out the petals. Dry flat. Paint on the leaves, stalk and bud using white petal dust mixed with clear spirit and a little mint green colour. When paint is dry, assemble the fuchsia petals on the plaque or cake as shown with a little green royal icing.

Stick the green frame on top with royal icing. Add butterfly, if wished.

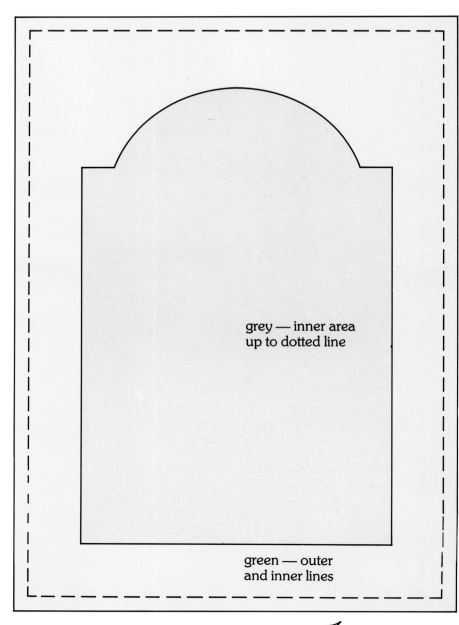

grey — inner area
up to dotted line

green — outer
and inner lines

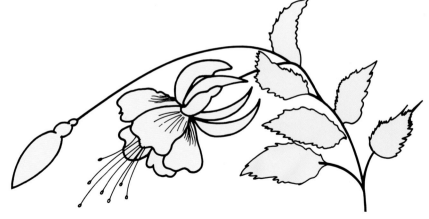

Moulded Sugar Work

Moulding sugar

This sugar is used for eggs, bells and moulds.

10ml (2 teaspoons) cold water
225g (8oz/1 cup) caster (super-fine) sugar

Add water to the sugar in a bowl and mix with a small fork or palette knife. The consistency should be that of damp sand.

If making coloured items, put the colour into the water. It will take some experimenting to be able to judge the shade of the resulting sugar. This sugar will keep in a covered plastic container for several days.

Sugar lumps

Use tiny chocolate or sugarpaste moulds to make sugar cubes for a special dinner party or afternoon tea. Try to make them about the size of half a teaspoon (2.5ml).

Snowman and Christmas tree

The snowman was moulded from a 10cm (4in) chocolate mould. Turn out two halves. Let dry and stick together with royal icing. A sugar-paste scarf, hat and features are added. The tree is moulded in two halves from green sugar in a chocolate mould and stuck together when dry. Pipe garlands using royal icing and wrap a strip of red paste around the pot.

Easter egg

Make egg with a plain egg mould. Pipe on decoration in blue royal icing with a No 0 tube.

Sugar mice

Mould in pink sugar using a commercial mould. Attach string tails with royal icing when dry.

Frilled Christening Cake

This christening cake features layers of delicate frills. The bas relief baby is covered with a hand-painted quilt.

Add frill to outer edge. Model baby's head and shape body. Roll out a large piece of paste and cut into a rectangle for quilt and blanket. Paint on flowers. Add frilled edge and ribbon.

To apply Garrett frill to cake: scribe a mark on the cake where frill is to be placed. Work lower frill on each corner of cake. Apply second row on each corner. Frill the final continuous row. (See also page 21.)

Bas Relief

Bas relief is a technique which will produce a shallow relief or two- or three-dimensional design on the surface of a cake or plaque. It can be straightforward or complicated, depending on the design chosen. Until proficient in this technique it is preferable to work on a plaque so that mistakes can be more easily corrected. This will have an added benefit as this technique is quite time consuming in that the plaque can be kept as a momento long after the cake has been eaten.

The principle is similar to a runout where the picture is created by completing the background first then working gradually forward.

For bas relief a combination of sugarpaste and Mexican paste is used.

The sugarpaste is used principally for building up the main body of the design. The Mexican paste is more pliable and is used to drape, cover or clothe the shapes or figures. As both pastes are quite soft, a modelling tool can be used to form depressions, creases and curves.

The main object is to mould and attach the clothing or covering in such a way that it appears to encircle the figure or shape, giving a three-dimensional effect.

For finishing details a number of techniques are used. Add the features and any patterning or shading on clothing with dusting colour and paint (food dye). Pipe in the hair. Paint the immediate foreground, add flowers and grasses using the Mexican paste.

Basic shapes for the bas relief baby on the Christening cake.

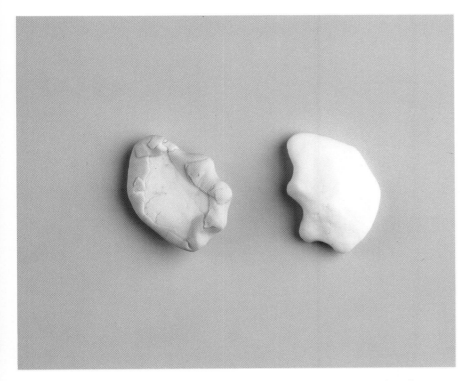

To give a more rounded effect in bas relief make the basic shape from white sugarpaste. When dry, cover the thinly rolled paste in the chosen colour for the design. The body of the baby is made using this technique.

Finished baby covered with a painted quilt.

Rabbit Plaque

There are several variations on the basic bas relief method. Instructions for the Clown Cake can be found on pages 124-127.

This form of bas relief is very different from the clown and little girl. Trace the pattern and scribe onto the plaque (or cake surface). Brush egg white over the outline and build up the rabbit from a mixture of half sugarpaste and half Mexican paste. Make an eye socket and indentations in the ears. Blend pieces into each other using a greased dresden tool.

Make templates of the basic body parts; head and ears in one piece, lower half of body, and two legs. Roll out some brown paste and cut out head and ear piece. Brush egg white onto the surface; place in position. Stretch the paste to touch the plaque. Indent ear cavity and eye socket. Use a porcupine quill or small darning needle to texture the fur. Add stamens as shown. Brush ear holes pink and place a white eye into the socket. Paint pupil black.

Use the same method for all the other visible brown areas, then dress in jacket, shirt and bow tie made of appropriately coloured paste.

Template

Claygun. This piece of equipment was designed for pottery work but has now been adopted by sugarcraft artists. Marzipan, flower paste, sugarpaste and Mexican paste can all be used in the clay gun. Soften paste with white fat as it compresses under its own weight. Place a small amount of paste into the syringe for best results.

Little Girl Plaque

This little girl was made using the bas relief technique to make her three-dimensional, then assembled on a sugarpaste plaque. The plaque can then be removed and kept as a souvenir when the cake is cut. Figures for this technique can be drawn freehand, or copied from greetings cards, picture books, comic books or children's colouring books.

Template

Finished plaque

Plaiting. Extrude some paste which has been coloured a suitable shade for hair. Divide into three strands. Pinch together at top and plait. Finish off by pinching together; make a bow of paste and attach to base of plait.

The little girl is made in the same way as the clown on page 124. The pieces that appear furthest away are put on first; legs before shoes and dress before the apron. Hair is made with a clay gun as explained opposite.

Courting Couple Plaque

The bas relief figures can be assembled directly on the cake top, or on a plaque which can then be removed and kept as a souvenir of the occasion. The pretty frills (see page 21) around the cake have been hand-painted to match the girl's dress.

Finished plaque

Template

Courting Couple Cake

This cake would be ideal for an engagement cake, small wedding cake or for an anniversary. Choose an oval or round cake and cover with white sugarpaste. Bas relief is used to make the courting couple three-dimensional.

As the couple are worked straight onto the cake, it must be firm and dry. Cut out a large circle for the moon. Slightly depress girl's head where the boy's head is to be placed on top. Roll long sausages for fence posts. To complete background; paint grass, make flowers and paint with a very fine brush. Use the same flower pattern as on Garrett frill on girl's dress.

Clown Plaque

This clown can be made in any colour combination. Assemble directly onto a cake or attach to a plaque. The paste used is a mixture of half Mexican paste and half sugarpaste. Sugarpaste alone is used for the basic shape.

Flatten the backs or cut one sausage in half lengthwise to form two posts. Cut out lower edges of dress and tips of toes. Roll out and attach lower rail. The lower part of the legs are angled and should appear to protrude from the plaque. Model legs in sugarpaste, cutting away more and more paste as they recede into the picture. Drape with clothing. Pipe hair with stiff royal icing.

Make second rail. Build up upper bodies. Build up the boy's left shoulder slightly as this shoulder and arm will protrude more from the plaque as the arm is placed around the girl's shoulders.

Model skirt and trousers and position seated on rail. Make arms and cover with white and pink sleeves. Add creases and folds. Moisten and place in desired position. To add finishing touches; paint flowers on dress, stripes on trousers. Add bow to dress.

Clown Cake

A charming bas relief clown on top of an oval cake suitable for a child's birthday party. Make the clown in the colours shown, or use the child's favourite colours.

Cover a medium size oval cake in pale lemon sugarpaste. Leave to dry for 1-2 days, then assemble clown straight onto the surface. Directions for the clown are given overleaf. Pipe the border on the board using a No 57 tube. Roll out blue paste and cut into strips 5mm (¼in) wide. Divide top into eight and use egg white to attach one end of the ribbon. Twist and attach other end, draping into scallops. Finish with a large plunger blossom at top of each scallop.

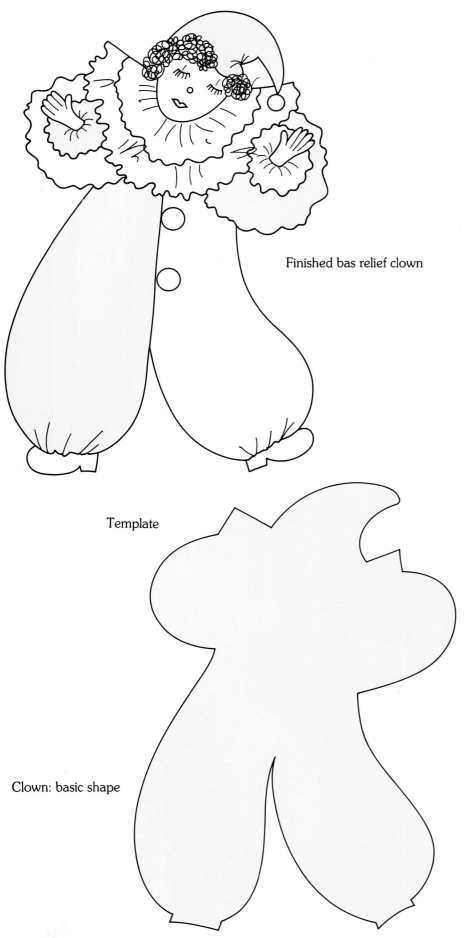

Finished bas relief clown

Template

Clown: basic shape

Roll out some white sugarpaste 3mm (⅛in) thick. Cut out the basic shape using a template made following the pattern. Stick to cake surface or plaque with egg white.

Roll out some blue paste to 1.5mm (¹⁄₁₆in) thick. Cut out the first (blue) trouser leg freehand or following the leg of the pattern. Cut the trouser leg approximately 15mm (½in) wider than the leg at the bottom so there is enough paste to pleat. Cover to stop from drying out.

Pleat the wider end of the trouser leg, and using a little egg white, stick as shown.

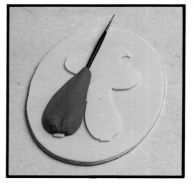

Brush a little egg white up both sides of trouser leg, pull over and up to give balloon effect. Stick a paintbrush or similar down the top of the trouser leg.

Repeat for second (white) trouser leg. Let dry for about five minutes, then squash the top ends downwards so the arm and neck ruffs can go into position neatly.

Roll out some blue paste and follow template to cut a strip for sleeve. French pleat with your fingers along one edge to make a fan shape. Check against the template to be sure it will be large enough.

Attach to clown with egg white. Trim if necessary. Repeat for white sleeve. Make cavities in the sleeve centres with a modelling tool. Make two holes with a small ball tool for pompoms on trousers.

Roll out some white paste and cut into two narrow strips for ruffles. French pleat and attach as shown.

Roll out some white and some blue paste. Cut out one white and one blue round using a small cutter. Frill with a cocktail stick and place on a piece of foam. Use a modelling tool to cup them. Make a hole with the end of a paintbrush for wrist.

Make hands as shown. Roll a ball of flesh coloured paste; cut in half. Model each into a pear shape and flatten the wide end. Cut fingers and thumb, place on foam and cup with a ball tool.

Place wrist frills and hands into position. Mould face, using the template to check size and shape. Stick into position with egg white. Use a ball tool to make a hole for the nose and make the mouth with a curved tool.

Roll out some blue paste and cut around hat template. Place hat into position. Pompoms are a cone shape, stuck into holes in trousers and on the hat by the ruff. Use golden yellow paste put through a clay gun or metal sieve to make hair. Place in position with egg white. Mould boots from brown paste.

To paint face, brush pink petal dust on cheeks. Add a piece of pale pink paste for nose. Paint mouth a dark pink and eyes brown using a fine paintbrush. Finally use silver petal dust mixed with clear spirit to paint pompoms and detail on ruffs, etc.

SUGAR FLOWERS

Sugar flowers make the prettiest cake decorations. Here is an array of piped and moulded flowers to try, with many artistic ways of displaying them, such as delicate piped flower baskets and bouquets.

Piped flower cake. *This design can be adapted for many different occasions, and is suitable for any sized cake. It can be used on sugarpaste, as shown, or on a royal-iced cake.*

Pipe a large assortment of royal icing flowers in various sizes and shapes. Leave to dry thoroughly. Mark a circle on top of the cake.

on top of the cake. It should be about 5cm (2in) smaller than the diameter of the cake, and the easiest way to mark it is to place a suitably-sized thin cake board on the surface and mark around it with a scriber or a hat pin.

Fill a medium-sized piping bag with green royal icing and attach a leaf tube, or cut to a W-shape. Pipe leaves around the marked circle,

covering 5-7.5cm (2-3in) at a time and attaching the flowers as you go. Try to get a good flow of colour around the ring. When finished, use a No1 piping tube with pink icing to pipe embroidery around the flowers. Pipe around the base with a No2 tube and either green or white icing. Attach 1cm (⅜in) ribbon around the side, tie the bow and curl the ends.

Piped Flowers

Piped flowers can be made in many different varieties, shapes and sizes. Flowers can either be piped onto flower nails, or onto squares of wax paper stuck onto the work surface. Cut several 2.5cm (1in) squares of wax paper before beginning. Flowers are piped with a petal or flower tube, and these are available in right-handed and left-handed versions. Piping perfect flowers takes a lot of practise to know how to maintain the correct pressure and learn when to release pressure. The icing must be fairly firm, so that the flowers hold their shape, made by adding 15ml (3 teaspoons) powdered egg white to 50ml (2fl oz/¼ cup) water and 450g (1lb/4 cups) icing sugar. Extra egg white makes the icing stronger, lighter and it will set more quickly.

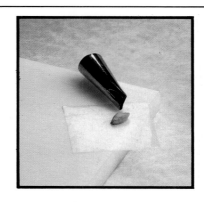

Basic piped blossom. Place a square of wax paper on the work surface. Place the petal tube in the end of a bag and fill with stiff royal icing. The thicker end of the tube should always be towards the centre of the flower. Start off piping, using your wrist to give the flow to the petals, and keeping an even pressure. Pipe a tight horseshoe shape.

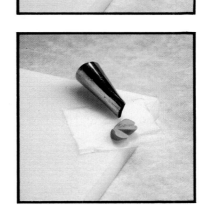

Rotate the wax paper and pipe the second petal.

Rotate the wax paper and pipe the third petal. You should have covered two-thirds of the circumference of the flower. If not, the petals are either too fat or too thin.

Rotate the wax paper and pipe the fourth petal.

Rotate the wax paper and pipe the fifth petal, release pressure and carefully lift the bag away. Pipe a small dot in the centre using a contrasting colour and a small tube. (See also pages 132-134.)

Sugar Flowers

This section is about making and using flowers in sugarcraft. It explains how to make all kinds of sugar flower – piped, moulded, cutter and wired – and how to use them in cake decoration. Many new and different techniques are covered, and every idea is illustrated with clear, step-by-step colour photographs.

There are many different ideas for using sugar flowers, and new and different styles for cakes. As with all aspects of sugarcraft, many techniques described here are simply guidelines. There are few rules for cake decorating, and most skills come down to a matter of personal preference. Experiment to find the methods that work best for you, and the ideas and designs that you most enjoy creating.

Of course, to be a good sugarcraft artist you will need an all round general knowledge of decorating skills. Beautiful sugar flowers and sprays need to be displayed on expertly covered and decorated cakes. Experiment with the different covering mediums, remembering again that there are very few rules. Sugar flowers can look equally good on sugarpasted or royal iced cakes.

The style of flowers used on a cake will depend on the overall style and design of the cake. When designing a cake, first consider the occasion, the number of portions required and the shape. Although most people prefer round or square cakes, there are now many different-shaped tins on the market.

Hints and tips

Flower paste and modelling paste are affected by the warmth of your hands. A cake decorator with very warm hands would need to use a slightly firmer paste than someone with cold hands.

Always colour pastes with paste food colourings, not liquid ones, which will change the consistency of the modelling pastes. Add the colour using the end of a cocktail stick, and always use a new coctail stick whenever more colour is added.

After colouring flower paste or sugarpaste, put it in a plastic bag and return it to the refrigerator for a few minutes. Kneading in the colour will make the paste warm and stringy, and it will be difficult to use without chilling.

Many colours, particularly yellows and reds, will deepen on standing, so colour a paste a shade lighter than the desired finished colour.

An alternative method of colouring flowers is to make them all white, cream or a pale shade and then petal dust to the desired shade when dry.

Petal dust is a powdered food colouring based on cornflour (cornstarch), which can be mixed in with the petal dust to obtain a lighter shade.

When using petal dust or lustre colour on flowers, be sure that the cake is boxed or removed from the room, or the fine dust may float through the air and discolour the cake covering.

Flower paste should be rolled as thinly as possible so that the petals will be translucent and natural looking. Paste can be rolled out on a thin film of white fat (shortening) or on a light dusting of cornflour

(cornstarch). Experiment to find which one works best for you.

When doing double frilling as in an orchid throat or carnations, the paste should be slightly thicker than usual or it will not frill successfully.

If using cornflour (cornstarch) to dust the work surface, place it in a square of butter muslin tied in a bag, or use a pepper pot for a miniature flour dredger.

Colour is perhaps the most important factor in the look of a celebration cake. To some extent this is dependent on fashion, particularly with wedding cakes. Because many brides now wear ivory, cream or pastel-coloured dresses instead of white, it is becoming more popular to cover the cake in a shade to match the wedding dress, instead of with pure white icing.

If using dark or vibrant colours on the cake, make only the smallest flowers of the spray in the darkest shade. Larger flowers must be pale or they will look heavy. Coloured ribbon bands or bows, or ribbon loops in the sprays, can add additional bright colour.

Again, there are very few rules about colour. Blue is often very cold, but can be made warmer when used with peaches or pinks. Lemons and

greens look very fresh and spring-like, and work very well on cakes. Use your eye and experiment to see which colours you prefer.

All flowers can be used either wired or unwired, depending on the style of the spray. In a South African-style spray every component must be wired, but in an Australian-style spray the larger flowers would be unwired and inserted into the base on the cake. Practise making the various sprays shown to discover which ones work best for your style of decorating.

Hints and tips

Roll out only enough paste to cut two or three petals at a time. Flower paste dries out quickly, and if too many petals are cut at once it will be difficult to frill, shape or mould them.

Try to obtain examples of the flowers you are making from a garden or florist, particularly when making a new variety.

It is not necessary to purchase every available flower cutter. Metal cutters can be bent to different shapes with fine pliers.

Cutter flowers can be made by using cardboard templates of the petals. Place the template on the rolled-out paste and cut round it with a modelling knife. This is a time-consuming method but useful if only a few flowers are being made.

When cutting out petals, the edges may look ragged. To avoid this, place the cutter on top of the rolled-out paste and apply enough pressure to cut through the paste. Turn the cutter upsidedown and gently run your finger along the edge of the cutter. Push the paste through and lift the cutter carefully away from the paste.

Piped flowers and foliage must be made from stiff icing or they will collapse. Add more icing (confectioner's) sugar to make the icing firm.

Never insert wires directly into the cake. Either place in a posy pick or insert them into a piece of sugarpaste on the cake surface.

When making crystallized flowers, take care to use flowers which are safe to eat. Never use flowers which have been grown from bulbs. Consult a florist or a reliable reference book about the suitability of a flower or plant,

and if in any doubt do not use it on the cake.

Buy inexpensive fabric flowers to practise making up and wiring sprays. Fabric flowers are easier to work with than sugar flowers, and time is saved by not having to mould flowers.

When making a wedding cake, ask for details of the bridal bouquet and make the flowers for the cake to match.

Piped Flowers

Piped flowers are made using petal or flower tubes which go up in size from 56 to 60.

Flowers that stand off the cake are made by folding the wax paper in half before starting. Pipe half the flower on each side of the fold. Dry with the folded paper at a 90° angle against the side of a box or tray.

The rose is the most popular piped flower. See page 134 for step-by-step illustrated instructions.

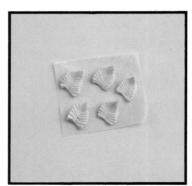

After piping flowers and leaves onto squares of wax paper, transfer them to a tray or board and leave to dry.

Dahlia. Rotate the nail anticlockwise while piping small close round petals. Work four layers of petals, going inwards until the centre is filled. As you reach the centre pipe smaller petals.

Blossom or Forget-me-not. Rotate the nail anticlockwise; press, stop pressing, pull round. Keep the petals small and short and the flower even. Ease the last petal in and pull off.

Primrose. Pipe anticlockwise with the thick side of the tube touching the paper. To form a heart shaped petal use the following action: press, release, pull down, press, pull up, release. Pipe five small petals.

Daffodil. Pipe six long petals; pull a paintbrush handle down the centre to make a point. Centre may be a trumpet with the same tube in a clockwise direction, or pipe three circles with a No 0 tube one on top of the other. Pipe a frilled edge and stamens in the centre of the trumpet.

Daisy or Clematis. Starting at the centre of the nail pipe to the outside with the thick end of the tube touching the paper. When the tube almost reaches the outside of the nail pull back to the centre and take off. Pipe long thin petals until the flower looks finished.

Lily-of-the-valley. Pipe a curved stem first, then small piped lines curving downwards. Pipe a small dot at the top and larger bulbs towards the bottom. Pipe very small dots around the base of each small bulb.

Pansy. Mix colours on a palette first, then place in the bag. Pipe two top petals anticlockwise, then one on each side. Keep the fine side of the tube tilting upwards. Pipe a yellow or brown centre.

Sweet pea. Pipe the stems first and the green leaves and tendrils. With two-tone icing, first pipe the large petal at the back with the side of the tube touching the nail. Then pipe a small petal on top and a bud in the centre. The green calyx may be piped afterwards with a No 1 tube.

Piped Roses

Attach a square of wax paper to nail and hold in left hand. Hold the petal tube vertically with the broad end of the tube towards the centre of the nail. Keep the broad end on the paper and lift the narrow end of the tube until the bag is at a 90° angle.

Finish by turning the tube flat and pulling away. For the third petal, repeat as for the second petal beginning slightly higher up the cone, and starting at the opposite side.

The tube is held horizontal and upsidedown for the fourth petal. Lift the tube up and turn it over while moving the nail clockwise.

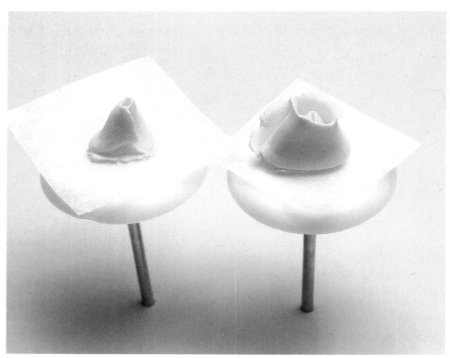

Lift the tube from the paper and turn the nail clockwise to make a cone. When you have made a complete rotation, turn the tube so that it lies flat and pull away. For the second petal, hold the bag at 90° angle with the broad end of the tube at the bottom. Begin part way up the back of the cone, turn the nail clockwise and pipe a band around the cone, lifting and lowering as you go.

The fifth and sixth petals are made in the same way, each slightly overlapping the one before.

The finished rose.

Cocktail Stick Flowers

These flowers will add height to a cake. Stick them straight into the cake. If the cocktail stick forms the stem of the flower, colour it green with food colour before piping. Pipe leaves along the stick starting at the bottom.

Add the flowers, which can be copies of real flowers or imaginary ones. For the white or yellow bell flowers, use a No1 tube and make a circular movement to create the bell shape. (See Greenhouse cake on page 55.)

Sunflowers. Pipe the flowers onto wax paper on a nail, using a small flower tube and stiff yellow icing. Hold the tube at right angles to and almost touching the nail. Squeeze and pull the petal sharply towards the centre. Work a circle of petals leaving a space in the centre. Fill the space with brown dots. When dry stick the flower to a cocktail stick which already has leaves attached.

An assortment of different piped flowers used as top and side decorations on cakes.

Flower Basket

A beautiful display of wired piped flowers with ribbon in a piped basket.

Wired Piped Flowers and Basket

Use 24-gauge flower wire. Make a hook at one end. Fill a bag fitted with a No 4 tube with firm peak royal icing. Insert the hook into the tube and squeeze while withdrawing the wire to coat the hook with icing. Push the hook into the tube a distance equal to the height of the flower you plan to make. Allow to dry. For the rest of the piping use a flower tube. Never insert the wires directly into a cake or use wired flowers on children's cakes.

Leaves. Lay a piece of straight wire on wax paper. Fill bag with two shades of green icing and cut the end into a V-shaped point. The more of the bag you slice off, the larger the leaves will be. Pipe a leaf, making sure the tip of the leaf covers one end of the wire. For smooth long leaves, move the tube quickly. For wavy leaves either move the bag slightly from side to side or up and down. Experiment to get different effects.

Carnation. Hold the wire vertically and the icing bag horizontally with the narrow end of the tube uppermost along the centre. Turn the wire clockwise while applying pressure to the bag and moving the tube up and down. Continue until the flower is the size you require. Dry for a few minutes. Snip the petals with small scissors. Pipe the calyx with a bag cut for making leaves.

Piped basket. Tape oval pattern to the side of a bottle and tape wax paper over the pattern. Pipe basket work with a No 2 tube. Neaten the top edge with piped interlinked S-designs. Pipe a handle over the bottle, also with an interlinked

Daisy. Pipe a short blob onto the wire with a No 4 tube. Allow to dry. With a No 1 tube pipe a series of pulled dots in yellow to cover the blob.

Fill a small flower tube with white icing. Hold the flower upsidedown and pipe the outside petals with an out and in motion.

S-design. The handle should extend as far around the bottle as the basket extends. When dry, remove the pieces from the bottle and fill basket with flowers arranged in sugarpaste. Stick the handle in place with royal icing.

Yellow rose. Pipe a long blob on the hook with a No 4 tube. With the narrow edge of a flower tube held uppermost hold the icing bag horizontally next to the icing blob. Twist the wire clockwise while applying an even pressure to the bag. Pipe all the way around, then gradually lower the tube to form a bud. Stop the pressure when your fingers have twisted the wire as far as they can.

Pipe the second petal with the narrow end of the tube leaning slightly away from the vertical. Pipe around while twisting the bud clockwise. Lift the tube up and then down to complete the turn. Pipe the third petal in the same way, starting opposite the end of the second petal.

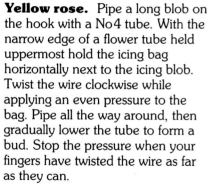

Round basket. Dust the basket nail or small round pot with icing (confectioner's) sugar, then cover with a little flower paste.

Depending on the size of the weave, different size tubes may be used. Starting at the bottom, pipe basket weave – a long line with short lines crossing it – (the downward line should be one size smaller than the cross line). Pipe round the base of the basket, then the sides. Keep the tube in the same position and pipe loops to join the coloured lines. Leave to dry overnight. Take the basket off the mould. If if doesn't come off easily it needs more drying time. Insert green sugarpaste.

The handle can be milliner's wire covered with piping. Stick it to the bottom of the basket with icing. After 24 hours when the icing is set it can be picked up by the handle.

Pipe flowers on 26-gauge wire. When dry, arrange flowers inside basket. In an arrangement try to have the height built up in steps on each side. Curve a few flowers over the edge. Use different size flowers plus some buds.

For petals four and five, hold the bag horizontally, with the broad end of the tube touching the base of the flower and the narrow end at the left. Your hand should have the palm facing down.

Squeeze while turning your hand holding the bag through 180° and twist the flower clockwise with the other hand. Each petal should overlap the preceding one slightly. Pipe the calyx with a bag cut in a V-shape as for piping leaves.

Below right:
Fill the basket with white foam or white paper turned upsidedown. Cover with small piped green leaves. Stick on flowers.

Below left:
Push a handle made with milliner's wire into the bottom of the basket. Place pale green flower paste on base in which to stick the wired flowers.

Left:
Put some sugarpaste inside basket and pipe small green leaves over the base. Arrange wired flowers putting buds at the top and edges with the larger flower in the centre as a focal point.

Moulded Flowers

There are two distinctly different ways of making modelled flower paste flowers – hand-moulding and using cutters. Most sugar flower sprays include both types successfully, although if entering a competition check the schedule carefully to see if this is allowed.

Pulled flowers. Hand-moulded flowers are usually known as pulled flowers, and they are the easiest moulded flowers to make. No special equipment is required, only a sharp modelling knife and wooden modelling sticks. Pulled flowers can be made in miniature or life-sized. The smaller the piece of paste used, the smaller the flower will be.

Cutter flowers. Cutter flowers are made by rolling out the flower paste and cutting it out with a cutter before shaping or frilling. Metal and plastic flower cutters are available in many different shapes and sizes. However, it is not necessary to acquire every cutter, as a skilled decorator can learn to bend cutters using pliers and to shape the paste for a particular petal once it has been cut from another petal shape.

Always try to make cutter flowers by working from a real flower. Pull off a petal and find a cutter which is close to its shape. If no cutter is available, either bend another cutter or make one from a sheet of thin metal.

Flower Paste

All of the moulded flowers in this section have been made using this recipe for flower paste. However, there are many variations on this recipe, so experiment to find one which suits you. Remember that flower paste is affected by climate, and if you live in a very humid place, then you may need to add more cornflour (cornstarch) and reduce the amount of icing sugar.

> 425g (14oz/3½ cups) icing (confectioner's) sugar, sifted
> 60g (2oz/½ cup) cornflour (cornstarch)
> 15ml (3 teaspoons) gum tragacanth
> *or*
> 10ml (2 teaspoons) gum tragacanth and 10ml (2 teaspoons) carboxy methyl cellulose
> 25ml (5 teaspoons) cold water
> 10ml (2 teaspoons) powdered gelatine
> 10ml (2 teaspoons) liquid glucose
> 15ml (3 teaspoons) white fat (shortening)
> white of one large egg, string removed

Sift together the sugar and cornflour in the bowl of a heavy-duty mixer. Sprinkle over the gum tragacanth, or the gum tragacanth and carboxy methyl cellulose.

Place the mixer bowl over a large pan of boiling water. Cover the top with a dry cloth, and then with a plate or cake board.

Put the water in a small glass bowl and sprinkle the powdered gelatine over it. Leave to sponge.

Half fill a small saucepan with water and place over low heat. Bring to just below the boiling point. Place the bowl of sponged gelatine, the container of liquid glucose and the beater from the mixer in the water. Heat until the gelatine is clear. Remove the bowl of gelatine from the pan and stir in the liquid glucose

and the white fat. Stir until the fat is melted.

When the icing sugar feels warm, take the bowl off the pan of boiling water, dry the bottom, and place on the mixer. Remove the beater from the other pan, dry, and assemble the mixer. Add the gelatine solution and the egg white to the sugar. Cover the bowl with a cloth, and turn the mixer to the slowest speed. Mix until all the ingredients are combined and the paste is a dull beige colour.

Turn the mixer to maximum and beat until the paste is white and stringy. This will take 5-10 minutes. Remove the paste from the bowl and place in a clean plastic bag. Place the bag in an airtight container and refrigerate for at least 24 hours before using. If planning to store the paste for a few weeks, put it in four or five small bags and open one at a time.

To use the paste, cut off a small piece, add a smear of white fat and dip into some egg white before working. The warmth of your hands will bring the paste to a workable, elastic consistency. Remember that the paste dries out very quickly, so keep it covered at all times and never cut off more than a very small piece. Certain colours, particularly reds and violets, may change the consistency, so it may be necessary to add more white fat and egg white.

Quick flower paste

This paste is easier to make, but the flowers will not be as delicate.

> 225g (8oz) commercial sugarpaste
> 5ml (1 teaspoon) gum tragacanth
> white fat (shortening)

Knead the sugarpaste and gum tragacanth together, adding a small amount of white fat to get an elastic consistency. Store and use as for the previous recipe.

Carnation

Cutters. As cutters are expensive, store them carefully packed in a box to prevent them from getting bent out of shape. Keep them clean, and if you wash them, dry immediately. Plastic cutters are less fragile, but take care not to damage them with sharp modelling tools.

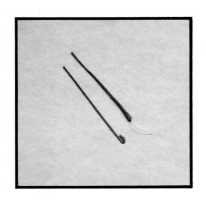

Make a hook in the end of a piece of 26-gauge wire. Cut the tip from a stamen, fold the stamen in half, and attach it to the hook with fine wire. Tape from the end of the hook for about 5cm (2in) down the wire. Run scissors along stamen cotton to curl it.

Cut and frill two more petals. Thread the first one onto the wire, then turn upsidedown so that the petal falls in a natural shape onto the head. Repeat with the second petal. Gently mould the base of the petals onto the wire. Leave to dry.

Roll out some coloured paste. Carnations look best when made in pale pink or cream paste and then petal dusted to a darker shade. Cut with a carnation cutter. Use a sharp modelling knife to make small cuts all around the scalloped edge at regular intervals. Frill with a cocktail stick. Keep turning the paste while working, and apply quite a lot of pressure to get the right effect.

For the calyx, make a cone from green paste. Cut five petals with a knife, then cut to the points with scissors. Thread onto the wire and gently mould round the base of the petals.

Put some egg white over half of the frilled petal. Thread the prepared wire through the centre of the petal and fold up the other half to make a fan shape. Brush some egg white on the right-hand third and fold over. Turn and repeat on the other side. Mould gently onto the wire.

Petal dust the dry carnation by working from the outside to the inside to give a greater density of colour on the frilled edges. Alternatively, for a softer look, dust from the inside to the outside. Finish with leaves made from floristry tape or flower paste.

Shallow Dish Flowers

Scabious. Lightly grease a shallow dish. Roll out blue paste very thinly and cut two circles with a round cutter. Frill the edges with a cocktail stick and place one on top of the other in the dish. Roll some strips of white paste, frill, and arrange in a ring in the centre. Make some tiny cones and attach to the centre with egg white. Place a few stamens in the centre of the flower. When dry, dust the centre with green petal dust.

Fully blown rose. Cut a green calyx and place in the shallow dish. Choose three sizes of rose cutter, and cut five petals with each one. Soften and cup all the petals. Arrange in three layers in the dish, starting with the largest petals and finishing with the smallest. Place yellow stamens in the centre. Petal dust the dry flower.

Christmas rose. Cut a green calyx and place in the shallow dish. Cut five white petals using a rose or Christmas rose cutter. Soften, cup and assemble as for the poppy. Position yellow stamens on a base in the centre. When dry, lightly dust green around the base and stamens.

Briar rose. Cut a green calyx and place in the shallow dish. Roll out white paste and cut five petals with a heart cutter. Assemble as for the poppy. Place a ring of yellow flower paste in the centre and fill with yellow stamens. Texture a piece of paste with some tulle and place in the very centre.

Poppy. Cut a green calyx using a small rose calyx cutter and place in the shallow dish. Cut five red petals with a rose petal cutter. Soften the edge and cup onto foam. Place the petals, one at a time, onto the calyx and stick with a little egg white. The fifth petal should be placed overlapping the fourth and tucked under the first. Make the centre from a ball of yellow paste. Attach

two rings of black stamens. Position a green paste stigma in the centre.

Water lily. These flowers can be pink, white, lilac or yellow. Make two or three shades of paste before beginning, so that the flower is darker in the centre. Use a water lily petal cutter to cut about ten petals from the palest paste. Soften, cup and place in the dish. Cut more petals from slightly darker paste and assemble in another layer on top. Continue until the desired effect is achieved. Attach stamens in the centre. Cut the leaf with a water lily leaf cutter. Soften, vein, and then soften the edges with a cocktail stick.

Sweet Pea

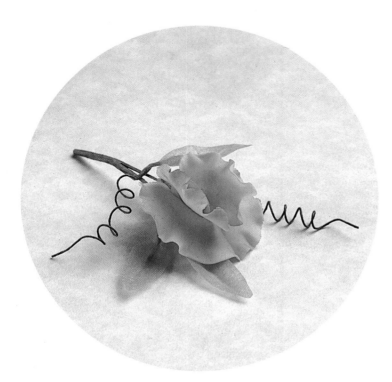

Cut a petal using a sweet pea cutter. Frill with a cocktail stick, cup each side and attach to the previous petal with egg white. It should look a little like a butterfly.

Cut out another petal with the larger sweet pea cutter. Frill, vein the centre with a modelling tool, and attach with egg white.

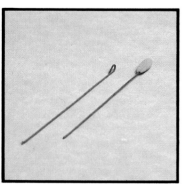

Use pliers to make a small hook in a piece of 26-gauge wire. Dip the hook in egg white, then cover with a very small piece of paste.

Cut a pale green calyx using either a small calyx or star cutter. Attach by threading the wire through the centre and pulling up.

Roll out some pale coloured paste and cut the first petal using either a small rose petal cutter or a pansy petal cutter. Attach with egg white down one side, place the first stage into the centre and stick the two halves together. Mould onto the covered hook.

When the flower is completely dry, dust to the desired colour with petal dust or lustre colour.

Phalaenopsis Orchid

Many of the beautiful orchids opposite are made in a similar way to the Phalaenopsis orchid.

The Phalaenopsis, or moth, orchid comes in white, pinks, lilac and green. If making coloured flowers, colour the flower paste in a pale shade of the chosen colour, as it is difficult to dust the assembled flower because of the shape. Roll out a small cone of paste very thinly, retaining the centre cone, cut the node in half, and slightly cup each half.

Make a former from thin metal, such as an empty drink can. The former should be slightly larger than the sepal cutter used. Roll out another piece of paste and cut the three sepals with the sepal cutter. Slightly soften the edges with a cocktail stick. Place each sepal in turn on a violet leaf veiner and gently rub over the paste with the index finger. Place the sepals on the metal former to dry.

Using a lip cutter, cut out the centre lip, positioning the node in the centre of the cutter.

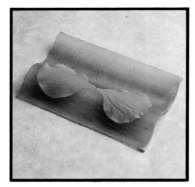

Roll out another piece of paste and cut one of the wing petals. Turn the cutter over and cut another, so that you have a pair of petals. Soften, vein and place on a curved surface to dry.

Slightly frill the two wing petals, then split the pointed petal in half. Roll the top petal into a thin tube and stick with egg white. Place in a small artist's palette to dry.

All pieces must be dry before assembling the orchid. Colour royal icing or softened flower paste to match the shade of the paste. Assemble the two wing petals, then attach the lip petal to the centre with royal icing. Mould a column with a cupped end and attach to the centre of the orchid. Petal dust and paint additional colour and shading to create a realistic flower.

More Orchids

A selection of exotic orchids to adorn your cakes.

Pansy orchid. Similar to the vanda orchid, these flowers are more like a pansy than an orchid, which is how they have acquired the name. Make with cutters and assemble as shown for the other orchids.

Cymbidium. This is a popular orchid for bridal bouquets and wedding cakes. It can be made with fixed petals or by wiring. Wired petals are easier to arrange in a finished spray. Practice is needed in shaping the tongue and lip to get a realistic look. Cymbidiums come in a wide range of colours, including very unusual green and dark gold shades.

Vanda orchid. These are easy to make using the wing petal cutter from the Phalaenopsis orchid. Assemble them in the same way. Although not common in cake decoration, they come in lovely shades of pink, peach and mauve, often with beautiful markings, and look attractive in sprays.

Cattleya. The easiest orchid to make, these are based on the same principles as the Garrett frill. Like the cymbidium, they can either be wired or unwired, with the wired orchids being easier to arrange in sprays. Catteyas come in shades of pink, lilac and white, and are traditional in American bridal sprays.

Dendrobium. The Dendrobium is commonly known as the Singapore orchid, and it is becoming very popular in sugarcraft. Although made with the same cutters as the cattleya, the petals are not frilled. It comes in many colours, although the ivory and pink is the most common one.

Alstroemeria

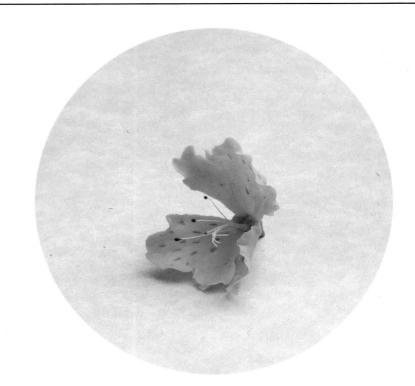

These large, trumpet-shaped flowers work well in sprays which are assembled directly onto the cake, as in Australian-style sprays which have a small sausage of sugarpaste as a base. They can also be wired. Alstroemeria come in many shades of yellow, red, cream and pink.

First make a former from foil, or use a small funnel. Cut a circle of foil and make it into a cone.

To assemble, place one petal in between two of the outer petals. Place the other two petals together at the top of the flower.

To make the petals, bend an azalea cutter with pliers to get the correct shape. Roll out some paste and cut three petals. Take each petal and vein with three lines. Frill the square end, pull a tiny lip in the centre, and curl over the edges slightly. Cup with a ball tool.

Assemble the three petals in the foil cone. Stick with a little egg white where they overlap.

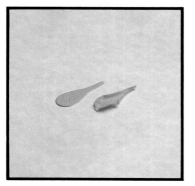

For the three inside petals, bend a freesia cutter, cut, and treat as for the outer petals.

Wire together three white stamens and then four brown stamens. Tape both sets together, and position in the centre of the petals. Petal dust the dry flower and paint in the markings on the petals. Attach a small cone of green paste to the base for the calyx. The cone could contain a piece of wire if the flowers are to be wired into a spray.

More Trumpet-Shaped Flowers

Rubrum lily. Roll out the paste using a paint-brush as for variegated ivy, (see page 150), retaining a thicker part. Cut out six petals, keeping a thicker piece at the base. Insert a wire into the thicker portion, and place the petals on foam, cupping slightly until dry. Twist the wires together and cover with floristry tape. Petal dust and paint on the dots with food colouring. For stamens, mould some paste onto the wire and dust.

Scarborough lily. Roll out some pink or red paste and cut three petals. Mark lines all over the petals with a veiner and soften the top with a cocktail stick. Assemble in a foil cone. Make three more petals and position these over the first layer. Position six stamens. Petal dust when dry.

Bridal gladiolus. Roll out some pale pink or peach paste and cut four petals with an azalea cutter. Soften, insert wires, and place over a small rolling pin to dry. Wire the petals together. Cut two more petals, soften, and attach to the flower. Position the stamens. When dry, petal dust the flower and cover the wires with floristry tape.

Azalea. Cut out a petal using an azalea cutter and slightly frill it. Place on a sponge and mark the centre vein using a veiner or cocktail stick. Shape the petal by placing it on the table leaning against a wooden stick. Make four more petals. Assemble the five petals in a fan shape on the table and stick together with a little egg white. Drop into the foil cone and then stick the fifth petal on top of the first. Position six half stamens and one three-quarter length stamen. When the flower is dry, petal dust and paint spots on the throat and a few on the petals.

Tiger lily. Cut out three petals from orange paste using an azalea cutter. Soften the edges, then arrange in a foil cone, leaving gaps between the petals. Cut three more petals and position on top of the first row. Stick tiny pieces of orange paste on the ends of some stamens and place these in the flower. Petal dust when dry and paint in spots with brown food colouring.

Daisy

Roll out some white paste and cut using a daisy cutter. Use a modelling knife to cut each petal in half.

Frill each half petal using a cocktail stick. Place onto a piece of foam and cup the centre.

Make a hook in the end of a piece of 26-gauge wire. Take a ball of green flower paste, make into a cone and roll out using a paintbrush. Cut with a small calyx cutter. Dip the wire into egg white and pull down through the centre of the calyx. Place a small plug of green paste over the hook.

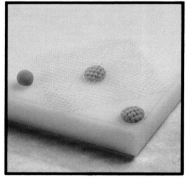

Put a small piece of dark yellow paste on the end of your finger. Pull a piece of tulle over the paste, then attach to the centre of the daisy.

Place the daisy onto the prepared calyx, sticking with a little egg white. Apply a little pressure to the centre with a modelling tool to ensure that it is firmly stuck.

Petal dust the centre and around the base of the petals with moss green colour. Daisies are attractive flowers for spring and summer wedding sprays.

Fuchsia

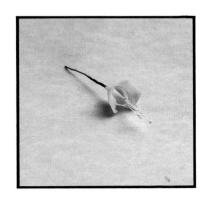

Attach to the cone so that they are opposite each other and cup inwards.

Cut, soften and cup three more petals with the same cutter. Attach to the centre with egg white so that they curve outwards. Dry for about 10 minutes.

Take four stamens and fold three of them in half. The one longer one is the stigma, and should extend about 5mm (¼in) below the others. Wrap a fine wire around the stamens, then attach to 30-gauge covered wire with floristry tape. Mould a small paste cone, then thread onto the wire through the centre. The thicker end should be at the wire end. Use a cocktail stick to mark three lines on the cone.

Using a different colour paste, make a cone and turn it into a hat shape. Use a fuchsia cutter to cut the petals. Vein the centre of each petal with a modelling tool. Cup the centre with a ball tool to make the cavity for the first stage. Pull the wire through the centre, attaching the outer petals to the inner ones with egg white.

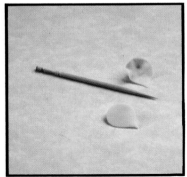

Roll out a piece of paste very thinly and cut two petals using a small rose petal cutter. Soften with a cocktail stick and cup slightly.

Petal dust the dried flower and stamens. Dust a little green on the base to represent the calyx. Fuchsias look best when arranged in hanging sprays. They come in many colours and an assortment on a cake looks very attractive.

Variegated Ivy

Ivy is an attractive foliage to include in sugar flower sprays, as it is small and comes in many shades of green. Variegated ivy is ideal, as its delicate shading blends well with most colours. These instructions are for variegated ivy: other ivies and foliage can be made in the same way and then coloured differently.

Colour the flower paste ivory or cream. Take a pea-sized ball of paste and squash it between your thumb and forefinger.

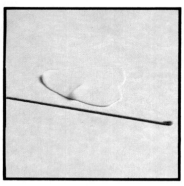

Using a small paintbrush or similar tool, roll the paste from the centre to the outer edge, keeping an area in the centre which is large enough to insert a wire into.

Cut out the leaf with an ivy cutter, placing the base of the cutter over the thickest part of the paste. Take a piece of 28- or 30-gauge wire and make a hook in the end. Dip the hook into a little egg white. Holding the leaf firmly between your thumb and forefinger, carefully insert the wire into the thick part of the paste.

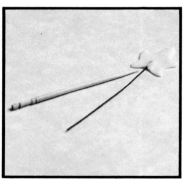

Secure the wire by carefully moulding the paste around it with your fingers or with a cocktail stick.

Vein the leaf using a violet leaf veiner on both sides. Dry on foam or crumpled tissue to create a natural shape. Do not dry flat, as the leaf will be stiff and unnatural.

Paint the dry leaf. The idea is to build up the variegation by using three or four tones of green. Dilute some moss green colouring with clear alcohol to make a weak coloured solution. Paint the leaf all over on both sides, working from the centre to the outside edge. Leave some cream on the edges. When dry, add a bit more colour and add some darker shading. Continue until a realistic variegation is created.

Christmas Cake

This royal-iced Christmas cake features an unusual spray of winter jasmine, ivy, holly and mistletoe. For the side design, pipe holly using green icing and a No1 tube, then pipe red dots for berries with a No0 or 1. Pipe a shell around the base. The top edge has small running scrolls piped with a No42, then overpiped with a No2. Wire the spray, adding red and green ribbon loops. Pipe an inscription if desired.

Pulled Flowers

Pulled flowers are hand modelled, using no cutters. Although most of the flowers have five petals, the examples on this page show that they can look quite different. Here is the basic technique for these flowers, making a basic blossom. These blossoms can be wired into sprays or used as filler flowers in other sprays.

Basic blossom. Shape a piece of paste into a cone. (The size of the piece of paste used determines the size of the flower.) Skewer the thick end into a cocktail stick or sharpened piece of dowelling. Make five equal cuts in the wide end using a sharp modelling knife. Remove the paste from the stick and shape each petal in turn. First, squash the petal between your thumb and forefinger. Pinch the end of the petal to slightly round the edges. Pull the end of the petal gently between your thumb and forefinger, with the thumb on top. Repeat the squash/pinch/pull technique on all five petals, making them all the same. Make a hook in the end of a piece of 28- to 30-gauge wire, dip into egg white and pull down through the centre of the flower. Mould the flower onto the wire and leave to dry. When dry, petal dust the flower.

Violet. Cut the cone into five petals, with one petal slightly larger for the tongue. Squash/pinch/pull all the petals, then soften the edges with a cocktail stick. Cup the petals on either side of the tongue using a ball tool. Attach the wire and leave to dry. Dust the finished flower with white and yellow, and add a fine line of yellow royal icing.

Bouvardia. Take a long, thin piece of white or pink paste and mould onto the end of a wooden stick. Cut four equal-sized petals. Squash/pinch/pull the petals to a slight point at the ends. Vein the centre. Mould the flower onto fine wire. For bouvardia buds, mould the paste straight onto the wire. Arrange into a clustered spray.

Frilled blossom.
Although not a specific flower, these can be made in various sizes and used as filler flowers in sprays. Make a cone of paste, mould onto a wooden stick and cut five equal-sized petals. Squash and pinch, but do not pull the petals. Instead, frill each petal with a cocktail stick. Mould the flower on 28-gauge wire. When dry, petal dust as desired.

Cymbidium orchid.
Cut the cone into six, with one petal slightly larger than the others. Frill the large petal, and squash/pinch/pull the other five petals. Attach the wire with a right-angled hook, and tuck the frilled lip in at the sides. Add an additional piece of paste to the centre and attach with egg white. Colour the dry flower as desired.

Stephanotis. Take a long piece of paste and mould it onto the end of the wooden stick. Cut five equal petals. Squash/pinch/pull each petal. Vein down the centre. Hook a 26-gauge wire and attach into the centre of the flower. Place a few fine stamens in the centre, and position a green star calyx when the flower is dry. Dust with a little green.

Lily of the valley.
Take a small piece of white paste and mould onto a small ball tool instead of onto a modelling stick. Cut six small petals. Squash/pinch/pull each petal, then mould the flower onto a 30-gauge wire or onto a stamen. Mould the buds directly onto the wire or stamen. Wire into spray.

Crystallized Flowers

Crystallized flowers are easy to prepare and make attractive decorations for cakes.

Roses, violets and fruit-tree blossom are the most suitable types for crystallizing. Choose the varieties carefully; never use any flower which has been grown from a bulb. The flowers should have just opened and must be completely dry. For soft-stemmed flowers such as violets,

cut off the stem and hold with fine-pointed tweezers.

Store crystallized flowers between layers of tissue paper in an airtight tin. If kept in a cool place, they will keep for several months.

Crystallized flowers look best when arranged in a little bunch, as shown here. Pipe on the stem with a No1 or No2 tube and finish the spray with a bow.

Designs using commercially prepared crystallized rose petals, violets and mimosa. Pipe the stems and leaves with royal icing.

Lightly whisk some egg white, and use a medium-sized paintbrush to completely cover the flower petals and calyx. Sprinkle the flower with caster (superfine) sugar. The sugar can be coloured to match the flower by mixing in a little petal dust.

Shake off any excess sugar and dry the flowers completely. Smaller varieties can be left to dry on kitchen paper. For larger flowers and for roses, wrap a piece of wire around the stem and dry hanging upside-down to avoid squashing the petals.

Traditional Bridal Bouquet

The flowers and foliage used in this spray are wired roses, carnations, stephanotis, freesias, gypsophila and variegated ivy.

Make the wired flowers and ivy, then assemble together with the ribbon and butterflies.

Start wiring at the bottom by taping together several ivy leaves. Tape in some stephanotis, freesias and their buds, add some ribbons, then tape in a rose and a carnation.

Continue wiring the spray, bending to an attractive curved shape. Add filler flowers and foliage where needed to fill out the shape.

Build up the spray with more roses and carnations, surrounded by stephanotis and freesias. Fill out the shape with gypsophila, and wire in ivy and ribbon loops.

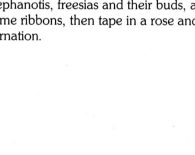

Finish the bouquet with ribbon loops, long trailing ribbons, and butterflies on wires fluttering over the cake. It may be easier to add the butterflies once the spray is in position on the cake.

Heart Wedding Cake

This two-tiered heart-shaped wedding cake features a sugar flower spray made to match the bridal bouquet.

The cakes are covered in ivory sugarpaste and decorated with scallops of lace in the shape of miniature bows. Piped embroidery is featured on the sides, while butterflies on fine wire flutter above the sugar bouquet on the top tier with two more positioned on the bottom tier (see page 115).

V-Shaped Spray

The V-shaped spray looks attractive on a round or hexagonal cake. This one is made using carnations, blossom, pulled flowers and ivy. Start by making two identical legs. Wire in buds, smaller flowers, foliage and finish with a carnation. The second leg should be a mirror image of the first, and an easy way to do this is to wire everything the same, then move the flowers to the other side of the spray. Wire the legs together. Make a posy with three carnations, tiny flowers and ribbon loops, and wire it in the centre.

Corsage

A corsage looks delicate on a small cake, or it can be used as a sugar-craft gift on a place card or instead of a bow on a wrapped package. The corsage shown here has a focal point of a single pink orchid, but another fairly large flower could also be used. Wire together with foliage such as ivy, some gypsophila, some ribbon loops and some bows with tails.

Straight Spray

This is probably the most common spray, and one of the easiest to make. Simply wire the flowers so that they increase in size, starting with buds and blossom and finishing with larger flowers and foliage, the largest at the bottom, adding 3mm (⅛in) ribbon bows. The pretty spray here includes roses, gypsophila, ivy and pulled blossom and stephanotis.

Posy

Posies are round sprays which look best placed in the centre of a fairly large round cake. A Victorian posy has a rose as the focal point. Round flowers such as roses or carnations work best in a posy, and there are usually either three or five main flowers included. Start by taping together three blossom. Add two ribbon loops. Keeping working in this way, going round in a circle adding larger flowers, buds and blossom, and taking care to keep the shape. When the desired size is reached, add some trailing ribbons and place in a frill or posy holder. Tape around the wires to cover them and attach to the holder.

Ribbons

Ribbons make attractive accessories to cake decorating. They are used in sugar flower sprays, to trim cakes and cake boards, and in ribbon insertion and banding (*see page 19*).

When using ribbon with flowers, it must be fairly stiff and not too wide. Bows and loops, with and without tails, make the prettiest additions to flower decorations.

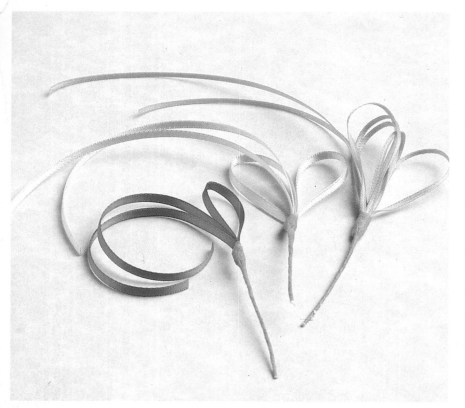

Australian-style Ribbon Loop

This spray is assembled directly into a small piece of sugarpaste stuck onto the surface of the cake using clear alcohol. The spray shown has been made using silk flowers, but it can also be made with sugar flowers. Follow an exact pattern, beginning with the ribbons. There should be a cross in the centre, then an eight-point star. Finish with two ribbon loops with tails. When the ribbons are arranged, place the flowers in position, sticking the wires firmly into the sugarpaste.

Peach Engagement Cake

This cake features an Australian-style spray made with silk flowers, which is assembled directly onto the cake covered in pale peach sugarpaste. The pressure piped doves (see page 40) and inscription are piped on the top. Finish off the sides with ribbon insertion (see page 19), embroidered bows and tiny flowers.

With Love
On Your Engagement
Day

INDEX

Advanced Royal Icing 48-87
Alstroemeria 146
Anemone Cake 36
Apple Cake 88
Applying royal icing 14
Applying sugarpaste 13
Australian-style ribbon loop 158

Baby, marzipan 91
Back to Basics 8-15
Banding, ribbon 19
Bas relief 118-127
Basic embroidery 42
Basic piping 38-39
Baskets, flower 136-139
Bee, inlay 35
Bells 110
   Filled 111
   Half 110
   Wedding 20
Birds
   Freestanding 70
   Pressure piped 40
Bridal bouquet, traditional 154
Broderie anglaise 22
   Plaque 23
Brush embroidery 37
Butterflies, lace 70
Buttons 109

Cameo plaques 104-105
Cards,
   pastillage greetings 114-116
Carnation 141
Cat Cake 25
Cat, sugarpaste 98
Characters, marzipan 90
Choosing colours 12
Christening Cake, Frilled 118
Christmas Cake 151
Christmas Cake, Runout 48
Christmas decorations,
   marzipan 34
Christmas Parcel Cake 33
Christmas tree 106
Christmas tree, cutwork 31
Claygun 120
Clown Cake 124-127
Clown, cutwork 32
Cocktail stick flowers 135
Cocoa painting 27-28
Collars, lace and filigree 73
Colouring royal icing 12
Colouring sugarpaste 13
Cornelli work 111
Corsage 156

Courting Couple Cake 122-124
Cradle, tulle work 61
Crimping 17
Crocodile, marzipan 95
Cross-stitch Cake 66-67
Crown Cake 80
Crown, filigree 81
Crown, winged 82
Crystallized flowers 153
Cutwork 30-35

Daisy 148
Decorating moulds 108
Decorations, Simple 16-35

Elaborate choir boy 103
Embossing 18
Embroidery
   Basic 42
   Brush 37
   Tube 43-45
Extension work 56-58
   Tulle 59

Father Christmas 102
Filigree 74-83
Filled bells 111
Fish, marzipan 95
Fisherman 94
Floating filigree plaque 78
Flower baskets 136-139
Flower paste 140
   Quick 159
Flowers, moulded 140-159
Flowers, piped 129, 132-135
   Piped Flower Cake 128
Flowers, Sugar 128-159
Fox Cub Cake 26
Fox, marzipan 93
Freestanding birds 70
Frill, Garrett 21
Frilled Christening Cake
   118
Frog, marzipan 96
Fuchsia 149
Fuchsia card 116

Garrett frill 21
Gelatine paste 89
Greenhouse cake 54-55
Greetings cards,
   pastillage 114-116
Gum arabic glue 89

Half bells 110
Heart Cake 16

Heart Wedding Cake 155
Hedgehog Candy Box 112-113

Inlay designs, marzipan 35
Inserts, lace 72
Ivy, variegated 150

Key, tulle work 61

Lace 62-73
   Butterflies 70
   Designs 64
   Inserts 72
   Parasol 86
   Two-tone 65
   Wings 68
Lace and filigree collars 73
Lettering 46
Little girl plaque 121

Making moulds 106
Marbling 13
Marzipan 9
   Cutwork 30-35
   Modelling 90-97
Marzipanning a cake for royal
   icing 11
Marzipanning a cake for
   sugarpaste 10
Mexican paste 89
Modelling 88-127
   Bas relief 118-127
   Marzipan 90-97
   Recipes 89
   Sugarpaste 98-105
Moulded flowers 140-159
Moulded sugar work 117
Moulds, decorating 108
Moulds, making 106
Mouse, standing 93
Mouse, sugarpaste 99
Mouse Wedding Cake 97

Orchids 144-145
Oriental stringwork 84-87

Painting, cocoa 27-28
Painting on plaques 29
Painting on sugarpaste
   24-29
Parasol, lace 86
Paste
   Flower 140
   Gelatine 89
   Mexican 89
   Modelling 89

Pastillage 89
   Greetings cards 114-116
   Hedgehog Candy Box 113
Peach Engagement Cake 159
Phalaenopsis orchid 144
Pink Birthday Cake 8
Piped Flower Cake 128
Piped flowers 129, 132-135
Piped flowers and basket,
   wired 137
Piped roses 134
Piping bag, making 15
   Using 15
Piping, basic 38-39
Piping shapes over a mould 41
Plaques
   Broderie anglaise 22
   Cameo 104
   Christmas cake 50
   Clown 124
   Cross-stitch 69
   Filigree cake 79
   Floating filigree 78
   Little girl 121
   Painting on 29
   Rabbit plaque 120
   Tube embroidery 45
Poppies, tulle work 60
Posy 157
Pressure piping 40
   Birds 40
Pulled flowers 152
Puss in Boots 100

Quick flower paste 140

Rabbit plaque 120
Recipes
   Flower paste 140
   Gelatine paste 89
   Marzipan 9
   Mexican paste 89
   Modelling paste 89
   Pastillage 89
   Royal icing 12
   Sugarpaste 13
Ribbon insertion and
   banding 19
Ribbons 158
Rose and leaf mould 106
Roses, piped 134
Royal Icing Work 36-47
   Advanced 48-87
   Applying 14
   Choosing colours 12
   Colouring 12

Recipe 12
Runout work 49-55

Shallow dish flowers 142
Simple Decorations 16-35
Sleeping Mouse Cake 52-53
Snooker Table 92
Snowman, sugarpaste 98
Sport Cake 105
Standing mouse 93
Straight spray 157
Stringwork, Oriental 84-87
Sugar Flowers 128-159
Sugar work, moulded 117
Sugarpaste 13
   Decorations 16-35
   Modelling 98-105
Swans 107
Sweet pea 143

Template, see individual cakes
   and plaques
Three-tier Rose Wedding
   Cake 71
Traditional bridal bouquet 154
Trellis side designs 67
Trumpet-shaped flowers 147
Tube embroidery 43-45
Tulle extension work 59
Tulle work cradle 61
Tulle work key 61
Tulle work poppies 60
Twenty-first Birthday Cake 62
Two-tier Cream Wedding
   Cake 58
Two-tone lace 65

Using a piping bag 15

Variegated ivy 150
V-shaped spray 156

Wedding Cake
   Bells 20
   Heart 155
   Mouse 97
   Three-tier Rose 00
   Two-tier Cream 58
Winged Crown 82
Winged Crown Cake 83
Wings, lace 68
Wired piped flowers and
   basket 137